THE MISSION OF JESUS

HOWARD BELBEN

The Mission of Jesus

LONDON
EPWORTH PRESS

© *Howard Belben* 1970
First published 1970
by the Epworth Press
All rights reserved
No part of this publication may
be reproduced, stored in a retrieval
system, or transmitted, in any
form or by any means,
electronic, mechanical, photocopying,
recording or otherwise, without
the prior permission of the
Epworth Press
Set in 11/13 *Baskerville*
and printed and bound by
The Garden City Press Limited
Letchworth, Hertfordshire
SBN 7162 0137 2

To my wife

AUTHOR'S NOTE

Except where otherwise stated, the New Testament quotations in this book are from *The New English Bible*, © 1961, by permission of the Oxford and Cambridge University Presses, and the Old Testament quotations from the *Revised Standard Version*, © 1946 and 1952, by permission of Thomas Nelson and Sons Ltd.

I am grateful to the Rev. H. J. Royston Emms and the Rev. A. G. Pouncy for reading the manuscript and making a number of useful suggestions.

Cliff College
Whitsuntide 1969

HOWARD BELBEN

CONTENTS

3 THE METHOD OF JESUS

INTRODUCTION

M A N Y Christians once assumed that nothing could halt the onward march of their gospel. The Church would advance from victory to victory until the whole world was brought to the feet of Christ.

Now, late in the twentieth century, the old optimistic missionary hymns are seldom sung. The spread of communism, the resurgence of the ancient faiths of the East, and the rise of humanistic philosophy and of secularism in the West, have checked the advance of the gospel, so that the number of non-Christians in the world is increasing faster than the number of Christians.

It is against this background that the Church considers its task of mission today. We are being driven back to first principles, and, although the modern world seems removed much further than any previous age from the world of the New Testament, it is to the New Testament that the Church must turn to find what these first principles are.

'Mission' is here understood as all that God has sent

us out to do. This includes both the spreading of His gospel and the serving of all men in their need.

Many books have been written on the life and on the teaching of Jesus, but not many on His mission. In these pages we shall not attempt to cover the whole life of Jesus, and we shall deal with His teaching only incidentally. Our concern here is to watch Him at work among men.

We all learn best by first watching the expert at work, and then putting into action what we have seen. In this book we shall be watching the greatest expert who ever lived, as He engages in the mission of God. It will then be for us to put into action what we have seen.

ONE

The Attitude of Jesus

W H E N we speak of a man's attitude, we mean something much more than physical posture. 'I don't like his attitude,' we say of someone aggressive or prickly. 'I prefer his attitude,' we say of another who is more gracious and tolerant.

Our attitude reveals our way of thinking about ourselves and others. The coy, the self-conscious, the timid, the fussy, the impatient, the awkward, the belligerent, are telling us something about themselves before they have spoken a word.

The Christian's effectiveness in mission can be greatly affected by his attitude. Because of the importance of this, we shall begin our study of Jesus at work among men by looking at His attitude.

(a) *He was sure of His calling*

Jesus was supremely confident. But it was not exactly

the characteristic we describe as self-confidence which he possessed. He was confident because He was sure of His calling; He knew that God had sent Him.

Armed with the power of the Spirit (Luke 4:14), Jesus has begun His startling ministry in Galilee. In his home town of Nazareth He has His first opportunity of speaking in the synagogue, and the passage He reads from Isaiah 61 begins: 'The spirit of the Lord is upon me, because he has anointed me; He has sent me to announce good news to the poor.' 'Today,' He says, 'in your very hearing this text has come true' (Luke 4:16-21).

In Capernaum the people want to keep Jesus to themselves, and press Him not to leave them, but He says, 'I must give the good news of the kingdom of God to the other towns also, for this is what I was sent to do' (Luke 4:43).

'Sent' seems to have been one of the favourite words of Jesus, and it is given special emphasis in the Fourth Gospel. It is worth looking up these references to Jesus' being sent by God: John 5:36,38; 6:29,57; 7:29; 8:42; 10:36; 11:42; 17:3,8,18,21,23,25; 20:21. In all these verses the word translated 'send' is the word *apostello*, from which our word 'apostle' comes. But this is only one of the Greek words used to convey this meaning, and in John another word meaning 'send', *pempo*, is used of Jesus' being sent even more times than this first word.

The sense in which Jesus was sent was, of course, unique. But this does not mean that being sent is something for Him, but not for the ordinary Christian. The Fourth Gospel tells us that Jesus directly linked

God's sending Him with His sending His disciples. In the High Priestly prayer He says, 'As thou hast sent me into the world, I have sent them into the world' (John 17 : 18); and to the disciples on the evening of the first Easter Day, 'As the Father sent me, so I send you' (John 20 : 21).

We do not call ourselves apostles, but we are 'sent ones' all the same, for the great commission to the apostles has been handed down to the Church. 'I have sent them into the world' applies to us, and we should not forget that Jesus said 'into the world' and did not say 'into the Church'. For too long the Church has been for some an escape from the world; but there is now a rediscovery of the Church's mission, and a fresh recognition that the world is God's world and that He sends us into it and not out of it (John 17 : 15). He sends us into it protected by the power of God's name (John 17 : 11).

So the Christian, like Jesus, can be sure of his calling. He stands in the world neither intimidated by its hostility nor arrogantly scornful of it. His is not the self-confidence that borders on brashness; it is the God-confidence of the one who knows that God has sent him.

There has been a crisis of confidence among Christians, conscious of living in a secular age. The morale of many is low, and their attitude in face of the world reflects the fact. One of our great needs is to recover what Jesus had : the confidence of one sure of his calling.

(b) He really loved people

The love of Jesus for men and women was so different from love as men usually understand it that the New Testament writers felt it necessary to find a Greek word little known in the world of their day, and free from any sordid or trivial associations, and to make this word, *agape,* their word for the distinctively Chistian kind of love, the love of Jesus.

Jesus loved His disciples with a persistent love that survived their slowness to learn and their tendency to let Him down. 'He had always loved his own who were in the world, and now he was to show the full extent of his love,' says the evangelist as he is about to describe Jesus' washing of the disciples' feet (John 13 : 1).

But it was not only the twelve disciples whom He loved. In John 11 : 3,35f. we see His love for one of His friends outside the immediate circle of the Twelve. 'How dearly He must have loved him!' said the Jews when they saw Jesus in tears as He met the party of mourners for Lazarus.

More remarkable than this love for His friends, however, is the love He showed to one who was about to reject His call, the rich young ruler. 'Jesus looked straight at him; his heart warmed to him'; or, as the Revised Standard Version puts it, 'Jesus looking upon him loved him' (Mark 10 : 21).

Most amazing of all is the love Jesus showed on the cross for those who put Him to death. When He cried out, 'Father, forgive them; they do not know what they are doing' (Luke 23 : 34), He was practising what He had preached to others in the Sermon on the Mount (Matthew 5 : 44). He was loving His enemies and praying for those who treated Him spitefully, and doing so under the hardest conditions imaginable.

There is nothing 'put on' about love like that. The words He spoke about God's love for the undeserving have the ring of truth, for they are all of a piece with the way He lived and the way He died. He really loved people, even those who hated and killed Him.

Most Christians feel incapable of showing love for the unlovely, and every minister is asked at some time, 'Is it possible to love those we don't like?' Apart from God the answer is probably 'No'. But the love we have been thinking of is not a merely human love. The clue may be found in Romans 5:5: 'God's love has flooded our inmost heart through the Holy Spirit he has given us'; and in Galatians 5:22, where love is named first in the list of qualities that are the harvest, or, in the older versions, the fruit of the Spirit.

I remember once attending a Bible Object Service to which children had been asked to bring objects named in the Bible, with the reference to the text attached. Each worker would then take an object and speak about it.

One boy had stuck a branch of a shrub in a flower-pot, and tied on some artificial fruit that he had made. The text was the one to which we have referred, Galatians 5:22. I have never forgotten the comment a friend of mine made when he took this object in his hand to speak about it. 'This fruit is tied on,' he said, 'but you can't tie on the fruit of the Spirit, though some people try to. If it's fruit, it has to grow from what's inside.'

We have all met people who try to tie on the fruit of the Spirit, who put on a show of love and the other qualities when in the company of those on whom they want to make a good impression. The real thing is shown when we are not in the company of those we are trying to impress. The real thing is a fruit of the Spirit.

So, if we are to have a share in the mission of God, we need an attitude of genuine love, God's kind of love. And only in the power of His Holy Spirit is that possible.

In saying this, we by no means imply that there is anything automatic about Christian love. It is both a gift and an achievement, involving an act of will as well as an act of faith. It is not only a fruit of the Spirit, but also a standard to aim at (I Corinthians 12:31-14:1).

In the sections that follow, we shall see some of the ways in which this love was revealed in the attitude of Jesus, and needs to be revealed in ours.

(c) He cared about unwanted individuals

We can learn a great deal about people from their attitudes to the misfits of society. Some bully them; some despise them; some laugh at them; some patronize them; some ignore them with embarrassment. The attitude of Jesus to those no one else bothered with was like none of those we have mentioned. His care for unwanted individuals is one of the most endearing things about Him.

At the outset of His ministry a leper kneels before Him, begging His help. Others will keep away. The most they might do is to speak a kind word, or leave a gift for him to pick up. Jesus can do more: He can heal him. To heal him there is no need to touch him, and men do not touch lepers if they can help it. Jesus is able to heal others with a word, sometimes a word spoken at a distance, so a word will do here. But Jesus, knowing how much it will mean to this man to have His healing

16

love mediated through a touch, stretches out His hand and touches him, saying, 'Indeed I will; be clean again' (Mark 1 :40f.).

In the Gerasene country a wild figure steps out from among the tombs, a man no one can control, shouting with uncouth cries, and bleeding from self-inflicted gashes. He is a creature no one can be blamed for avoiding, and we can imagine how wide a berth most people would give the area he haunts. But not so Jesus. Where others would dodge away with a shudder, Jesus faces his rage and calmly commands the unclean spirit to leave him (Mark 5 : 1-13).

In sharp contrast with the man in the tombs, a shy, self-conscious woman, who feels so painfully different from others because of the haemorrhages she has suffered for twelve years, trembles with fear when she finds that Jesus knows she has touched His cloak for healing. But she has no need to fear, for the warm sympathy of Jesus goes out to reassure her as she hears Him say kindly, 'My daughter, your faith has cured you. Go in peace, free for ever from this trouble' (Mark 5 : 25-34).

Other women who had reason to feel unwanted by society found Jesus ready to show that He cared : the woman in the house of Simon the Pharisee, unwanted because of her reputation as a sinner in the city (Luke 7 : 36-50); the woman at the well, drawing water at a time when there were no other women about, perhaps because her unsavoury reputation made other women shun her (John 4 : 5-42); the woman taken in adultery, who found to her surprise that the only person present who had a moral right to condemn her was the only one ready to shield her from her accusers (John 8 : 1-11); Mary Magdalene, whose tally of seven devils must have made her the most unpopular woman in town (Luke 8 : 2). Jesus had time for them all.

It was the same with the tax-gatherers, doubly unpopular because of the lavish rake-off they allowed themselves and, in the case of those in Judaea, such as Zacchaeus, because the taxes they collected went to the hated Roman conqueror. It cannot have been often that anyone outside their own circle wanted anything to do with them. But Jesus did, as Matthew (Matthew 9:9) and Zacchaeus (Luke 19 : 1-10) found to their joy.

Jesus had a mission to lonely, unwanted people, and so has His Church. Christians should be alert to the needs of the disabled, handicapped in body or mind, and of the shy, nervous, or inadequate personality. Time needs to be spent in learning how to understand and to help them, for some of them are sensitive people, and well-meaning bungling can do more harm than good. Some will sheer off if our approach is boisterous and pushing. But endless time and trouble are worth taking if we can help the unwanted.

The Miller of Dee's song has been the secret cry of thousands, especially in modern urban society :

> *I care for nobody, no, not I,*
> *And nobody cares for me.*

The order of the two statements is usually the opposite in the minds of those who feel themselves unwanted, however. They begin with the fact that nobody seems to care for them, so, as a defence against the pain they feel, they turn their faces away from company and, as a defence against being hurt still more, persuade themselves that they do not care for anyone either. They dare not face the fact of how deeply they need acceptance.

The modern problem of loneliness, especially in great cities and new towns, only occasionally comes into the limelight, as it did when the body of a woman was found and near her a diary in which she had written, day after day, simply the words 'No one came'. The problem affects, in old age, many who have no disability, handicap, or personality problem. The world has just passed them by.

Those who feel unwanted often become so used to it that when, at last, someone begins to care they are incredulous that anyone should bother with them. Sometimes they are pathetically grateful for any concern that can be shown and any help that can be given. And the hearts of such people are often wide open to the Christian gospel when they see that, because we are Christians, we care about them when no one else does.

Occasionally someone is heard saying that he thinks it is a pity that so many 'odd bods' are found in Christian churches. It is not a pity: it is a cause for joy. The presence of such people is one of the greatest tributes that can be paid to the Church of Christ. Others may have no time for them, but they know that Christians have, for Christians know that they must never say of anyone 'I can't be bothered with him'. The Christian knows that everyone mattered to Jesus, so everyone must matter to him.

(d) He was slow to condemn

The attitude of Jesus to those who had sinned was entirely opposite to the attitude of the Pharisees, who condemned sinners out of hand, who felt that any contact with them would bring contamination, and that the best way to teach them a lesson was to show one's scorn for them by keeping out of their way.

The contrast between the attitude of the Pharisees and the attitude of Jesus is most clearly seen in two of the incidents we have referred to in discussing Jesus' care for the unwanted.

When the woman who was a sinner in the city walked into the room where Simon the Pharisee was entertaining Jesus, and stood behind Him in tears, then impulsively washed His feet with her tears, wiped them with her hair, kissed them, and anointed them with ointment, Simon drew his own conclusions. If Jesus allowed her to do this to Him, then it must be because He did not know she was a sinner, and, if He did not know she was a sinner, then He could not be a prophet. Any good man would surely have driven her away (Luke 7 : 36 : 39).

The true situation was one that Simon had not contemplated as possible. Jesus was a prophet and a good man, and he knew of her sinful life, but He still allowed her to demonstrate her devotion in this embarrassing way. The Lord wanted to be able to confirm to this woman the certainty of forgiveness because of her saving faith, and He knew that if he brushed her aside with a scornful word of condemnation, He would be unable to help her further. So, instead of denouncing her sins,

He told Simon the story of the two debtors, and justified her demonstration of love as a proof that her sins had been forgiven. Then he said to her kindly, 'Your sins are forgiven. Your faith has saved you; go in peace' (Luke 7:40-50).

The same contrast is seen in the story of the woman taken in adultery (John 8:1-11). The moral indignation of Jesus was directed, not against the woman herself, but against the doctors of the law and the Pharisees who were using her in an attempt to trap Jesus into saying one of two things: either that she should be stoned, which would put Him wrong with the Roman authorities, or that she should not be stoned, which would put Him wrong with the Jewish authorities.

The answer of Jesus silenced them: 'That one of you who is faultless shall throw the first stone.' When, one by one, they had slunk out of the temple, He said to the woman, 'Where are they? Has no one condemned you?' Then, when she had replied, 'No one, sir,' He said 'No more do I. You may go; do not sin again.'

Neither of these stories implies that Jesus thought lightly about sin, or that He was permissive in the sense in which society is said to be today. The word he used to describe what the women had been doing is the word 'sin', plain and unvarnished. He told the woman taken in adultery not to sin again. What he said gives no encouragement to those advocates of situation ethics who argue that in certain circumstances adutery can be right, for he did not qualify in any way His plain direction not to sin again. But He was slow to condemn the sinner.

Jesus was much less concerned to judge what people had done in the past than to make sure that they had found forgiveness and were walking on a new road now. The parable of the Pharisee and the tax-gatherer is the supreme example of this. (Luke 18:9-14). The tax-gatherer had a worse record of wrong-doing than the Pharisee, who could recite an impressive list of the sins he had not committed and the good deeds he had to his credit. But it is our present position rather than our past record that matters more, and the one who went home that day acquitted of his sins and rightly related to God was the tax-gatherer, not the Pharisee, for the one with the bad record was the one who had cried out 'O God, have mercy on me, sinner that I am'.

Anyone engaged in God's mission to the world has need to learn from Jesus at this point, especially when he is dealing with individuals. The Christian does not treat sin lightly, and there is a time for speaking up plainly, as our Lord so often did. But the Christian who is easily shocked and quick to condemn will find it hard to win anyone from the wrong road.

Jesus could tell what was in a man (John 2:25), and His insight made Him able both to expose the hypocrisy of those who posed as better than they were and to understand the reasons why some were worse than they should be. If they were ready to be honest about their weakness, He would begin from there.

The Christian Church does not always make it easy for people to be this honest about themselves. The pharisaism that crept into Judaism can easily creep into any established religious institution that has standards to maintain. It is not easy to steer a middle course between the extremes of being, on the one hand, rigid and censorious, and on the other hand, culpably easy-going and permissive of wrong-doing. It is easy for church members, who feel their reputation as Christians to be at stake, to be much quicker to condemn than their Lord was, and to act as though He had never said to them, 'Pass not judgement, and you will not be judged' (Matthew 7 : 1f.).

William Gowland tells of an angry letter he received when prostitutes from Piccadilly began to attend the Albert Hall in Manchester. The writer, who had attended church all her life, said, 'At one time the Church was clean, but I think it is far from being clean today. How you can invite people from Piccadilly to be with respectable people I am unable to conceive.'[1] It does not seem that this Methodist had ever read the words of Charles Wesley's conversion hymn,

> *Outcasts of men, on you I call,*
> *Harlots and publicans and thieves,*
> *He spreads His arms to embrace you all,*
> *Sinners alone His grace receives.*

The modern world seems to put a particular strain on the tolerance of Christian people. To the things they have always felt should be condemned is added a list of other things that they feel in some way threaten the secure world of values they have known and accepted. Changing attitudes to authority, to the use of Sunday, to drink and drugs, to the length of skirts and the length of hair, to musical and artistic taste, seem all, in a way not clearly defined in the minds of most people, to constitute a threat to Christian values.

[1] *Militant and Triumphant,* Epworth Press, p. 44f.

We must not ourselves fall into the trap of condemning those Christians whom we feel to be intolerant. They, too, need understanding rather than judging. The reading of history and a little imagination would help them. It is worth remembering that the attitude of Jesus to the Sabbath and to sinners was felt by the Pharisees to constitute just such a threat to established values in their day. And presumably there was a day some time in the last 200 years when an older generation was scandalized by the new fashion of young men wearing short hair instead of long, as scandalized as some today are by the opposite.

Christians are not all intolerant. Some of those who are nearest to the spirit of Jesus are giving themselves to helping the alcoholics, the drug addicts, and the drop-outs of society with a vision and devotion that is not often found outside the Christian Church. They would have little hope of helping them if they did not accept them as people and if they were not, like Jesus, slow to condemn.

(e) He saw them as they might be

We referred earlier to the words used about Jesus in John 2:25: 'He himself could tell what was in a man.' In its context, this statement indicates that Jesus could see weaknesses in others that could not be seen on the surface. For this reason, the evangelist tells us, He did not trust Himself to many of those who gave their allegiance to Him when they saw the signs that He performed (John 2:23f.).

The words 'He could tell what was in a man' suggest, however, a wider meaning than this. When we say of someone, 'He has a great deal in him', we do not mean that he has a great deal of hidden evil in him, but rather that he has great possibilities. And Jesus was as skilled at seeing the possibilities as at seeing the weaknesses in men.

'You are ... You shall be ...' (John 1:42): the words of Jesus to Peter are worth pondering over deeply. ' "You are Simon, son of John. You shall be called Cephas" (that is, Peter, the Rock).'

Christians have long debated whether Peter, or faith such as Peter's, was the rock on which Christ would build His Church (Matthew 16:18). Whichever way we interpret the words, one fact is plain. The writer of the Fourth Gospel is giving us to understand that Jesus, when first He encountered Peter, saw in him not only the man he was, but also the man he would become. He saw in him not only the rough, insensitive, wavering fisherman he was in the Gospels (Matthew 14:29-31; 16:22f., Luke 9:32f.; 26:69-75, but Peter the apostle and leader who, from his first happy confession of faith at Caesarea Philippi (Matthew 16:16), moved forward, in spite of falls by the way, to become the strong, bold, staunch leader of the Church whom we see in the Acts of the Apostles.

In the same way, in Matthew, the civil servant sitting in the custom-house, Jesus saw the Matthew that would be, Matthew the disciple, ready to leave everything to follow Jesus, and eager to introduce his friends to the Lord (Luke 5:27-32).

Still more striking is what Jesus saw in John. In the early days Jesus had, as we should say now, nicknamed John and his brother James 'Sons of Thunder', or 'Thunderers', as J. B. Phillips translates it (Mark 3:17).

We have a glimpse of the characteristic that may have led Jesus to try to tease the two brothers out of being Thunderers in the incident recorded in Luke 9:54, when they were eager to call down fire from heaven to consume a Samaritan village that would not have Jesus because He was making for Jerusalem. The two brothers do not appear in a much better light when they appeal to Jesus to let them book the two places nearest to Him, fearing, presumably, that one of these places would be allocated to Peter, and that one of the brothers would be left out (Mark 10:35-40).

John and his brother do not appear very promising material in passages like these. But Jesus knew what it was in a man to become, and if (as many, though not all, believe) John the Thunderer is the Beloved Disciple of John 13:23; 19:26f.; 20:2-5; and 21:7,20-24, then he is one of the figures most associated with love in the New Testament, and one whose influence may perhaps be traced in the First Letter of John, with its tremendous statements about Christian love (I John 4:7-21). It took the unique insight of Jesus to see in the Thunderer such an apostle of love.

When we say that Jesus saw people as they might be, this is another way of saying that He believed His own gospel. 'I did not come to invite virtuous people, but sinners,' He said (Matthew 9:13), and He knew that lives could be transformed, that the worst could become the best.

If today we are to fulfil the mission that God has given us, we must believe the same. Too often we write off as hopeless those who seem to us a thousand miles away from Christian faith and character. We are inclined to say to ourselves, 'It's not much good hoping that *he* will ever become a Christian. He's too set in his ways (or too antagonistic, or too indifferent, or too much of a rogue). But that other neighbour of ours is a different proposition. He's a good sort. I'm sure he's not far from the Kingdom. It might be worth trying to win *him*.'

When Samuel Chadwick was a young lay pastor in the Bacup Circuit, the burden of his prayer was that God would give them a Lazarus, that someone would be converted whose turning from darkness to light would be so striking that people would see that God in Christ could truly raise men from the death of sin to the life of righteousness. God gave them their Lazarus.[1] Most of us have stopped asking for ours.

When a Church reviews its programme, it rightly looks round the fringes of its congregation and concentrates first on those whom it thinks of as 'likely prospects' : parents of Sunday School children, those who once came to church, those who will support the occasional special effort. It does not as often look 'beyond the fringe' and seriously set out to tailor its programme to serve and to win either the drop-outs of society at the one end of the scale or the happy, secure, successful pagans at the other.

The mission of God leaves no one out, and we must learn to see all men, as Jesus did, not as they are but as they might be.

(f) He did not easily give up

For those who are studying the mission of Jesus, the

[1] Norman G. Dunning, *Samuel Chadwick*, 1933 edition, pp. 44-46, 48-54.

story of the woman at the well of Samaria is particularly full of hints. One of the things that shines out from this story is the patient persistence of Jesus when she failed to grasp that He was talking in spiritual terms and thought He was talking about physical water (John 4 : 7-15).

Many would have been tempted to give up, but Jesus was ready to give time to helping this woman. He was prepared to wait by the well while she went to find her husband, and then to continue the conversation (John 4 : 16). When her reply gave Him the opportunity to indicate that He knew her story (John 4 : 16-18), she at once began to side-track Him on to less personal matters. But Jesus persisted. Courteously answering her question, He led her to the point that He wanted the conversation to reach (John 4 : 18-26).

Jesus did not easily give up with His disciples, either. We have seen how often a man like Peter lapsed. Yet Jesus never gave him up. Instead He persevered with him, prayed for him, and encouraged him. It must have been a wonderful moment for Peter when the Lord told him of His personal prayers for him : 'Simon, Simon, take heed : Satan has been given leave to sift all of you like wheat; but for you I have prayed that your faith my not fail; and when you have come to yourself, you must lend strength to your brothers' (Luke 22 : 31f.).

In the Sermon on the Plain, recorded by Luke, some manuscripts have the words 'without giving up hope of anyone' (in the older versions : 'despairing of no man') in place of 'without expecting any return' in the saying of Jesus about lending to others (Luke 6 : 35). Whether

28

or not Jesus said the words 'without giving up hope of anyone', the words fairly represent His own attitude.

This does not involve having faith in human nature as such. Even if we do not go so far as to say with Sir Herbert Butterfield, 'It is essential not to believe in human nature',[1] the Christian faith does not require of us, as some imagine, that we should have faith in man. Faith is not a good quality *per se*, irrespective of its object, for misplaced faith, such as a gullible people's faith in a tyrannical dictator, or a child's faith in a perverted seducer, can be disastrous. Christians should be less gullible than others, not more gullible, for it is they who have a realistic view of man as fallen and sinful.

The Christian view of man, however, as we have seen, also includes the possibility of his redemption and transformation, and the Christian should despair of no man. Not only does he try to see men as they might be, as Jesus did, but he does not allow that vision to be dimmed by discouragement. Like Jesus, he does not easily give up. He will not allow himself to forget that, though faith in man may be misplaced, Chistian love is 'always eager to believe the best, always hopeful, always patient' (I Corinthians 13:7; Moffatt).

In the Methodist ministry today there is a young man whose considerable gifts are already making their mark in the thinking of the Church. Less than twenty years ago he was a teenager, with no Christian home background, slipping completely out of the life of the Church. The leader of the Bible class he had attended

---

[1] *Christianity and History*, paperback editions, p. 47.

called to see him, with no success. He called again, with no success. He called again, every week, for three years. At last persistence was rewarded, and the slippery teenager felt he had said 'No' too often, and was shamed into returning to the class, where God spoke to him, faith dawned, and the call to the ministry came to claim his life and gifts.

It all happened because there was a man who, like Jesus, did not easily give up.

(g) He saw them as whole people

It has sometimes been said that there have been Christians whose attitude to man suggested they believed him to be nothing but a soul with ears. The taunt is not altogether unfair, for certainly there have been those whose only interest in people was an interest in them as souls to be saved.

The phrase 'a passion for souls' is not heard much these days. It represented an overwhelming concern that men and women should find eternal life in Jesus Christ. It has been the driving force of much, if not most, effective evangelism. Rightly understood, it is a vital part of the evangelist's equipment. But, standing on its own, it suggests a false division of man into soul and body, and an unjustified preference for the one as against the other.

Research into the meaning of the words used in the New Testament has shown that body, soul, and spirit are not there thought of as three different parts of man so much as three different ways of viewing man as a whole. We sometimes remind ourselves that we have bodies as well as souls, souls as well as bodies. Perhaps we should be speaking more exactly if we said that we were, rather than that we have, both souls and bodies. Jesus never forgot that men were both.

Thoughtfully He takes the tired disciples away for a rest after their preaching tour. There the hungry crowd that has followed them needs a meal, and He feeds the multitude. Neither the disciples nor the crowd will have felt that day that they were being treated as souls with ears (Mark 6 : 31-44).

The same thought for people's material needs is seen in the story of Jairus's daughter. The Lord's first concern when she has been raised to life is lest, in the excitement of the moment, others should forget her need of food. So He asks at once that she shall be given something to eat (Luke 8 : 55).

Every incident in the healing ministry of Jesus shows the same concern for men's bodies as well as their souls. Sometimes the two are clearly seen together, indicating that Jesus knew how closely man's physical and spiritual nature are interlocked. The paralytic is lowered down into the presence of Jesus in the crowded room where He is teaching. Men expect a healing miracle, but first they hear Jesus say, 'Take heart, my son; your sins are forgiven.' Only then does He say, 'Stand up and walk.' The crowd will have wondered, as we do, at the order of these sayings. It seemed that the man's prior need was the healing of his body, for surely this was why he had been brought. When Jesus first spoke about the forgiveness of sins, was it because He knew that a right relationship with God is more important than physical health? Or was it because He knew that there was a psychosomatic element in this man's affliction, and that the guilt he was conscious of was a cause of which the illness was a symptom? Whichever the answer, it was as a whole person that Jesus saw him, and as a whole person that He helped him (Matthew 9:2-8).

One day I was teaching a group of children in my church. The word 'soul' came into what was being said, and I asked what they thought it meant. At once, Kathleen, an alert ten-year-old, answered, 'God's little bit of us'. It was an attractive definition, coming from a child, but, of course, Kathleen was quite wrong. Neither the soul, nor anything else, is 'God's little bit of us'. God made whole people, and all we are is His. Jesus knew this, and His ministry showed that His mission was to the whole of life.

It is not only those who emphasize the soul at the expense of the body who limit the scope of God's message, however. In these days we more often meet those who seem concerned only with man's material needs than those who seem concerned only with his spiritual needs. The widening gulf between the 'have' and the 'have-not' nations has awakened consciences to the shattering facts of world poverty and hunger. The secularization of human life has been accepted and welcomed. Radical theologians have questioned whether 'man come of age' can be expected to have a religious faith.

It is as important that those who leave out man's spiritual needs should learn from the all-round ministry of Jesus as that those who leave out man's material needs should do so. Jesus gave the highest priority to the spiritual, even discouraging people from speaking of His healing ministry, partly, we may suppose, because of the danger that men would set physical needs above spiritual needs. He spoke with astonishing casualness about those who kill the body but cannot kill the soul (Matthew 10:28). He urged men to repent, forgave them their sins, taught them to think of God as their Father, instructed them in prayer, and commanded them to preach the gospel. He did not behave at all as though He thought men's material needs were more important than their spiritual needs. He saw them as whole people, and all their needs mattered to Him.

Those who emphasize either the spiritual or the material needs of men at the expense of the other need to see the total ministry of Jesus. His conception of salvation was broader in scope than the conception of many Christians today. On His lips the words 'save' and 'salvation' were used in contexts ranging from the forgiveness of sins (Luke 7:50) to the restoration of sight (Luke 18:42) and the transformation of character (Luke 19:8-10). He is a Saviour for the whole man.

(h) He spent Himself for others

Since the publication of John A. T. Robinson's *Honest to God* in 1963, the description of Jesus as 'the man for others, the one in whom Love has completely taken over'[1] has loomed large in the thinking of Christians.

To prepare for His mission Jesus spent forty days and nights fasting in the wilderness (Matthew 4:1-10). During that time He rejected the easy way to bring the world to His feet. He had set Himself already on the harder way he had chosen, and from the beginning of His ministry He set out to spend Himself for others.

[1] op. cit., S.C.M. Press, p. 76.

The strenuous Sabbath described in Mark 1:21-34 made it clear to the people of Capernaum how willing Jesus was to give Himself for men. There was first the synagogue service at which they heard Him teaching with a note of authority they had not heard from the doctors of the law. He went from the synagogue, with James and John, to the home of Simon and Andrew, where Simon's mother-in-law was in bed with a fever. After Jesus had healed her, she waited on them, and there were some hours of fellowship for them to enjoy together. But with the coming of evening and the end of the Sabbath the crowds began to arrive till, as Mark described it, the whole town was there, gathered at the door. There He stood, healing them, until all their needs were met.

Jesus had no doubt known what hard work was, as a carpenter. Now He was to know the doubly taxing life of an itinerant prophet, teacher, and healer.

Mark gives one glimpse of the demands made upon Jesus near the beginning of His ministry, when 'great numbers from Galilee, Judaea and Jerusalem, Idumaea and Transjordan, and the neighbourhood of Tyre and Sidon' crowded to the lakeside to see Him, and He had to ask His disciples to have a boat ready, to avoid his being crushed by the crowds, as sick people and those with unclean spirits were crowding in on Him (Mark 3:7-11).

At the end of a day of teaching the crowds by the lake, Jesus was so exhausted that he could sleep through a heavy squall at sea (Mark 4:1,35-41).

After the Twelve returned from their preaching and healing tour, people were coming and going all the time, so that they had no leisure even to eat, and he told His disciples to come with Him to a lonely place for a rest. But the crowds followed Him and, as always, Jesus gave Himself to them. He might justifiably have been angry at their giving Him and the disciples no peace, but 'his heart went out to them, because they were like sheep without a shepherd; and he had much to teach them' (Mark 6 : 30-34).

At the end of that day there was the feeding of the five thousand (Mark 6 : 35-44). Then Jesus sent the crowds away and the disciples across the lake and, of all things for such a tired man to do, went up the mountain to pray. But, Mark tells us, in the early hours of the morning the disciples were labouring at the oars against a head-wind, and Jesus made for them at once across the water because they were in need (Mark 6 :45-52).

Immediately they reached Gennesaret, Jesus was recognized. 'The people scoured that whole country-side and brought the sick on stretchers to any place where he was reported to be. Wherever he went, to farmsteads, villages, or towns, they laid out the sick in the market-places and begged him to let them simply touch the edge of his cloak; and all who touched him were cured' (Mark 6 : 53-56).

Unless we read a Gospel straight through, we do not see the cumulative effect of the tremendous demands Jesus met. For the sake of His ministry to men He was willing to lose sleep. More than once He spent part of the night in prayer (Mark 1 :35; 6 :46f.), and at least once, the whole night (Luke 6 : 12). He was ready to talk at night with a visitor, Nicodemus (John 3 : 1). For the sake of men He had left His carpenter's home, and at times there was nowhere for Him to stay (Matthew 8:20).

Though men made such demands upon Him, however, Jesus never indulged in self-pity. Four times the Gospels speak about Jesus sighing. But, when He did so, it was not because He was sorry for Himself, but in face of the Pharisees' demand for a sign (Mark 8:12), the need of the deaf man with an impediment (Mark 7:34), and the sorrow of the mourners after the death of Lazarus (John 11:33,38). The only tears we know He shed were not for Himself, but for the death of Lazarus (John 11:35) and for the city of Jerusalem (Luke 19:41-44), and He told the women who followed Him to the cross not to weep for Him, but for themselves and their children (Luke 23:27-31).

So it was without resentment or a feeling that monstrous demands were being made on Him that Jesus faced human need and spent Himself for others. Thus to give Himself away was life to Him. When, tired though He was with the journey, he still summoned energy to talk to a woman by a well about the water of life, He said to His disciples, when they returned, 'I have food to eat of which you know nothing. It is meat and drink for me to do the will of him who sent me until I have finished his work' (John 4:31-34).

We speak today about 'an outgoing personality'. Jesus was 'outgoing', not in the sense merely of being an extrovert, for He also loved solitude, but in the sense of being 'a man for others'.

It was not only in His ministry, however, that Jesus spent Himself for others; it was supremely in going through with the cross. When, as He lengthened His stride on the last journey to Jerusalem, and paced on ahead of His disciples, who followed, awestruck and fearful (Mark 10:32), we must not suppose that it was a merely human dread of the suffering of the cross that gripped His mind and made Him want to walk alone. Mark and Luke tell us that it was on that last journey through Judaea and Transjordan that He encountered human need and opportunity in the children, brought for Him to bless (Mark 10:13-16), the rich young ruler, filled with questioning (Mark 10:17-22), Zacchaeus, needing a friend and a saviour (Luke 19:1-10), and Bartimaeus, begging for healing (Mark 10:46-52).

Jesus had time for them all but, as He strode on towards Jerusalem after His encounter with them, He must have thought of all the others like them who still needed Him and who were silently calling Him to stay with them and serve them rather than go through with the cross. Perhaps He asked Himself whether, in steadfastly setting His face towards Jerusalem (Luke 9:51), He was, for the first time in His life, turning His back on human need.

But He still went on. It must have been because He was deeply convinced that this would be best for those He had come to serve. He had come to serve, and this He had been doing all His ministry, but He had come also to surrender His life, as a ransom for many (Mark 10:45). The four encounters along the road had brought before Him afresh the needs of children, of youth, of those in their prime, and of those on the scrap-heap of life. But, great though their human needs were, He believed He could serve them all best by the sacrifice of His life for them. So He went through with the cross, and spent Himself for others in the ultimate way. As was said of the Suffering Servant of God in Isaiah 53 : 12, He 'poured out His soul to death'. And in that act He was spending Himself not only, as He had done in His ministry, for the needy of His day, but for us and for all men.

What Jesus did for men in going to the cross was utterly unique, and we must guard against appearing to equate any human self-sacrifice with His. His suffering was infinitely more than an example: it was an atonement. But that it was also an example is made plain in I Peter 2 : 21. There it is cited as an example of how to bear undeserved suffering; here we are seeing it as the supreme example of self-spending for others.

It is not given to many Christians to spend themselves for others to the point of dying, though the second half of this century has had its Christian martyrs, as the well-known stories of the Congo and Ecuador show. But it is given to Christians to spend themselves for others in life.

In a generation that has more leisure than ever before, men are sometimes at a loss to know how to spend the free time they have. Many are finding that to do nothing, or to spend oneself seeking one's own ends, is unsatisfying. They are discovering the quality in man that William James called 'organic hardihood, disgusted with too much ease'.[1] But when for ease they substitute aimless activity, this, too, fails to meet their need. They

[1] *Varieties of Religious Experience,* Collins (Fontana), 1952 edition, p. 291.

need to be needed, they want to be wanted, and, especially if their daily work is work that carries no 'job satisfaction' with it, their frustration is acute.

In such a situation, many are beginning to ask what they can do for others. Help given to others, for whatever motive, is better than inactivity, but there is something out of joint about people seeking community service as a kind of occupational therapy for their own malaise.

There are many signs of a much more altruistic approach to helping people than this, however. In Britain, Community Service Volunteers, Task Force, Voluntary Service Overseas, and other agencies mobilizing those who wish to serve are not lacking in support. The Churches are looking outward to the world's need more than they have done for many years, and a variety of organizations have sprung up to take action on world poverty and hunger.

Though an increasing number of Christians are playing an active part in such organizations, such good service as we do can hardly be described as spending ourselves for others. Now and then we meet a Christian of whom this can be truthfully said, one who is prodigal in spending himself, who gives not just a due share of his money, but himself, to people in spiritual, social, psychological, or material need. But if the mission of Jesus is to be fulfilled in today's world, the Church must be ready to adopt the servant role He adopted, and it must become not exceptional, but normal, to find a Christian ready, like Jesus, to spend himself for others.

TWO

The Approach of Jesus

THE CHRISTIAN, by the very fact that He is a Christian, is committed to a share in the mission of Jesus, and has much to learn, not only from the attitude of Jesus, about which we have been thinking, but also from His approach to people.

(a) He offered men His friendship

We have seen already that the attitude of Jesus to people was one of love, a love that reached far outside the circle of His immediate disciples. But this was not merely the attitude of His heart: it showed itself in His friendly approach to men.

As we read the gospel story, we can detect that the disciples were always aware that Jesus was other than they were, so that, for example, Peter shrank in horror from the thought that Jesus might wash his feet (John 13:6,8). But it was not that Jesus set Himself on a pedestal. As far as He was concerned, they were His friends (John 15:14f.). He would rather call them that than call them servants, for He had taken them into His confidence. They had shared the same experiences together on the road, out at sea, and in the home; they had been together in fellowship and in service to others, and He did not hesitate to call them his friends, not excluding Judas Iscariot (Matthew 26:50).

It was through this offer of friendship that the disciples were drawn together into a team that became the nucleus of a Church, and, in one sense, it is natural that Jesus should have called these men His friends. What is more surprising and more wonderful is that He offered His friendship also to those with whom He might be thought to have had so little in common: the tax-gatherers and sinners.

It was Jesus Himself who said that He had the reputation of being the friend of these men, and that He was being criticized for it (Matthew 11:19). The Pharisees could not understand how He could choose to mix with and, even more surprising to them, choose to eat with bad characters (Matthew 9:10f.). Jesus had told those who questioned Him the reason: these were people who needed Him. 'It is not the healthy that need a doctor, but the sick', He told His critics. 'Go and learn what that text means, "I require mercy, not sacrifice." I did not come to invite virtuous people, but sinners' (Matthew 9:12f.).

The three parables of the lost in Luke 15 are in a context of the same controversy. The opening verses tell us that 'the tax-gatherers and other bad characters were all crowding in to listen to him; and the Pharisees and the doctors of the law began grumbling among themselves: "This fellow," they said, "welcomes sinners and eats with them." Luke specifically says that the parable of the lost sheep that follows was told in answer to Jesus' critics. It was the task of the shepherd to go after the missing sheep until he had found it. Whether the following parables of the lost coin and the lost son were told at the same time, we do not know, but they carry the same implication. When the lost are lost, what matters most is that they should be found, and when they are found there is cause for joy in heaven.

In the light of what Jesus said, it begins to seem less surprising to us that He offered His friendship to these bad characters, as the New English Bible calls them. What does seem wonderful is not only His willingness to spend time with them, but their obvious delight in His company. He seems to have done nothing to conceal the fact that He was befriending them because He believed they needed His help, yet, instead of their fighting shy of Him as a do-gooder, or resenting the implication that they needed putting right, they seem to have been genuinely attracted to Him and to have crowded round Him and enjoyed His company.

We wish we could have been there to overhear what He said to them and how He approached them, how He managed to convey acceptance of them without approval of their style of life. The expression on His face, the tone of His voice, the time He was willing to give them, must all have conveyed genuine friendship, with no patronizing and no strings attached, or they would never have warmed to Him as they did.

I once heard a friend of mine preach on 'the gospel

according to the enemies of Jesus'. One of his texts was the verse in Luke 15: 'This man welcomes sinners and eats with them.' Those who first spoke the words thought they were saying the most damaging thing they could about Jesus, but to us it is a part of the Good News. If Jesus did not receive sinners, what hope would there be for us?

The Lord's offer of friendship to the bad characters, however, not only gives us reason to admire Him; it also gives us reason to examine ourselves, and to ask ourselves to how many bad characters have we who, as Christians, are the representatives of Jesus in the world, made overtures of friendship.

The question of the Christian's attitude to the world is not an easy one. There is a friendship with the world that is enmity with God (James 4:4), but that is the friendship that drags us down. If we stand on a chair and have a tug-of-war with someone on the ground, we quickly find that it is easier to be dragged down than to pull someone up. We may remember that warning, but we must remember also that we can hardly hope to win others to faith in Christ unless we offer them genuine friendship.

Let me quote from one of the most experienced university missioners in Britain, John R. W. Stott. He has written: 'Why is there this frightening gulf between the churches and the masses? I will tell you. It is because the ordinary Christian is not mixing with non-Christians. From some experience of university missions, I would say that an indispensable condition of the "success" of a mission is that Christian Union members have large numbers of non-Christian friends . . . We are the light of the world; and the light must not be hidden under a bucket. We are the salt of the earth; and yet we prefer the snug safety of the salt-cellar. We are meant to be leaven, and it is the function of leaven to spread in the dough . . . Every Christian should be "the friend of publicans and sinners". Jesus received them and ate with them. They had access to the house where He was, and He welcomed and entertained them. Are we following in His steps?"[1]

Most active Christians are so busy that they find it hard to find time for deep, rewarding friendships of any kind, and friendship with those far from Christian faith is crowded out altogether. So was Jesus busy. Yet He found time.

(b) He started where they were

When Jesus approached people, He started where they were and found a link between their interests and His truth.

The first two to be called as disciples of Jesus were fishermen who were working with their nets when the moment came for Jesus to ask them to join Him. Starting where they were, with fishing uppermost in their minds, He said, 'Come with me, and I will make you fishers of men' (Mark 1 : 16f.).

The woman at the well of Samaria had come there to draw water, and, starting where she was, He used water as an illustration of the life He could offer (John 4 : 7-15).

Men came to tell Jesus about a cruel act of Pilate,

[1] *The Christian Graduate*, Vol. 12, No. 1, March 1959, p. 5.

44

and, starting from where they were, He led them on to see the need of repentance (Luke 13 : 1-3).

All the parables illustrate the Lord's way of finding a landing-ground in men's minds and linking what He had to say on to the things in which they were interested : homes, families, coins, farms, vines, wheat, weeds, seeds, food, pearls, buildings.

Few things are so important in our Christian mission as finding a link with people's interests. Christians do not always realize how ignorant of and uninterested in the Christian faith great numbers of people are. To begin with religion is to invite them to switch off, just as we switch off when people begin to talk about a subject on a quite different wave-length from our own. If we doubt whether this is so, let us imagine that we have our wireless set tuned in to Radio 3 one evening. We hear the announcer say that the next talk is to be on the subject of, let us say, 'The Logical Positivists' Rejection of Metaphysics'. We go across the room to switch off, but, as we go, we hear the speaker begin by saying, 'I went to church last Sunday and the Vicar said . . .' Every Christian would leave his wireless on when he heard that, even though he may not be interested in the subject of the broadcast, for the speaker has started by finding a landing-ground in the Christian's mind.

We need to face the fact that many around us begin with as little interest in the Christian faith as we may have in the logical positivists' rejection of metaphysics. Our one hope of a hearing is beginning where they are.

This is not as tall an order as we might think. In a common cultural background, in the common background of what has been in the papers, or on the wireless or television, in a common concern about the state of the world, thte Christian has a community of interest with almost everyone he will meet.

We do not suggest that those who engage in the mission of Jesus should sit down to prepare a short list of opening gambits to trot out to everyone they meet as a way in to the subject of religion. Jesus approached no two people alike, for no two people *are* alike. But His heart was filled with the love of God and compassion for men, and His mind was filled with the concerns and the interests of men, and bridges were constantly thrown across from His heart and mind to theirs.

(c) He listened to what they had to say

Jesus was a good listener. When He approached men and women, and when they approached Him, we find Him again and again listening to what men had to say before He began to teach them.

Nicodemus comes as an inquirer at night, and Jesus lets him do what he has come for: make his statement and ask his questions (John 3:1-15).

When the Twelve return from their tour, we find Jesus listening to them as they tell Him what they have been doing. A little while after, He is listening to their suggestions as to what can be done with the hungry multitude. Then, in the next incident recorded, He is asking them what men think about Him and is listening to their answers (Luke 9:10,12f.,18-20).

After the resurrection, the two on the road to Emmaus are encouraged to tell the Risen Lord of all their hopes and disappointments before He begins to speak to them from the Scriptures (Luke 24:13-27).

We shall not be of much use to the mission of Jesus unless we learn to be good listeners. There are three reasons why this is so.

The first is that a part of our mission is to help people in any way we can, and one way to help them is to listen to them, for many people are like corked-up bottles needing more than anything else someone to uncork them, someone just to listen to them—and drink in whatever comes out of the bottle.

The second reason is that, unless we let people have their say, they will be restless when we are having ours. We must all have had the experience of wanting to say something but not being able to get a word in edgeways. If people cannot get a word in edgeways because we are doing all the talking, they will certainly not be tuned in to what we are saying.

The third reason follows on from what we have said earlier about the importance of starting where people are. We do not know where they are until they tell us, and to listen in a percipient way, looking out for the little distress signals that are going up from the other person, noticing where the sensitive points are in their life, is to be half-way to seeing where the mission of Jesus can begin relevantly for them. If, as we have said, no two people are alike, and no two people are to be treated alike, that is a very good reason why the Christian, engaged in the mission of Jesus, should be a good listener.

(*d*) *He sought the root of their problems*

Jesus never skated over the surface of people's lives. Nor

did He assume that what appeared to be their need was, in fact, their paramount need.

The man lowered down through the roof of the house where Jesus was preaching was suffering from paralysis. But, as we saw when we were discussing this story as an illustration of the way he saw men as whole people, Jesus did not see this man's need only at the level at which others saw it. Others in the room would have said that ill-health was that man's one great problem, but Jesus went to what perhaps He could sense was the root of his trouble, and dealt first with the paralytic's feeling of guilt with the words, 'Take heart, my son; your sins are forgiven' (Matthew 9:2-7).

The rich young ruler felt a need in his life, but did not know what it was. He kept the commandments, but still felt something needed putting right. Jesus looked beneath the surface and sought the root of his problem. The young man's sense of values was wrong. He was rich, and his riches had not been surrendered to God. He was rich, while others were poor, and it had not troubled him. So Jesus went to the root of the matter for him (Mark 10:17-22).

The lame man at the pool of Bethesda may well have been surprised when Jesus, seeing him lying there, asked him, 'Do you want to recover?' The man might have asked what Jesus thought he was doing there in the crowd of sick people if he did not want to recover. But Jesus knew that he had been ill for a long time. And Jesus knew that when a man has been disabled, as this man had, for thirty-eight years, the adjustment from helplessness to having to do everything for himself would not be easy. He had been unable to work for

48

nearly forty years. If he was cured, he would have to go out the next day and look for work—at his age. Perhaps this is why Jesus asked the question, inviting the man to face up to whether he was prepared for the changes that would be involved for him if he recovered (John 5:2-9).

None of us possesses the unique skill of Jesus in finding the root problem beneath the surface problem that people present to us, but we can do something with the insight we have. A knowledge of modern psychology can help, though there are few matters in which it is so true that a little learning is a dangerous thing. Insight grows with experience, and spiritual insight grows with spiritual experience. We shall need much tact, and we shall have to be careful not to probe too much and not to jump to conclusions too quickly; but, if we are seeking the root of people's problems, we shall often be able to help people to see that behind many an intellectual problem lies a moral problem, behind many a social problem lies a personality problem, and behind many a material need lies a spiritual need.

(e) *He took their questions seriously*
Some Christian workers, in their eagerness to get to the root of people's problems, try to dig down too soon and will not spend time answering people's questions. It was not so with Jesus.

We have already seen that Jesus listened to what men had to say. He did more: He took what they had to say seriously and answered their questions, even when they were loaded questions asked with sinister intention.

If we read Mark 12:13-34 carefully, we shall see

how seriously Jesus took the questions of the Pharisees, Herodians, and Sadducees, although He knew that some of these questions were designed to catch Him out.

We have another instance in the story of the woman at the well of Samaria in John 4:16-26. As we have seen, the matter she raised about the right place at which to worship was probably raised at that point to side-track Jesus from the subject of her personal life. But the Lord did not brush the question aside with a rebuke to the woman for changing the subject. Instead, He took the question at its face value and gave a serious answer, telling her that the spirit in which we worship is more important to God than the place in which we worship.

The lawyer in Luke 10:25-37 who asked a question about eternal life was putting, Luke tells us, a test question; but Jesus, as always, took it seriously. Later, when the man tried to vindicate himself with the question 'And who is my neighbour?' Jesus gave him an answer in the form of the unforgettable parable of the Good Samaritan.

Everyone engaged in Christian mission knows that we can seldom argue anyone into being a Christian. But this does not mean that we are to ignore or brush aside the questions we are asked. Sometimes people ask them to vindicate themselves, like the lawyer in Luke 10, but this does not justify us in assuming at once that every time people ask us difficult questions about the Christian faith it is a smoke-screen put up to evade the challenge of the gospel.

There are genuine intellectual problems in the minds of a growing number of people, and they expect us to be prepared to give an answer to every man who asks us about the hope that is in us (I Peter 3 : 15). The young Christian may often find himself out of his depth, and he certainly needs to remember the limits of what argument can achieve, but, if we will never attempt to answer people's questions, they will soon infer that we have no answers to give.

To be equipped to answer the questions men ask will involve fearlessly thinking through our faith. It will mean getting to know our Bibles and understanding basic doctrine as thoroughly as a young Marxist or Jehovah's Witness knows his. There is no easy escape from the demand of this, but, if Jesus took men's questions seriously, so, with His help, must we.

(f) *He sometimes asked favours of them*

Sometimes, though not often, a part of the early approach of Jesus to people was to ask them a favour.

The first thing the Lord said to the woman at the well was 'Give me a drink'. The astonishment she registered, the evangelist tells us, was due to the fact that He, a Jew, was asking drink of her, a Samaritan woman, although Jews and Samaritans did not use vessels in common (John 4 : 7-9).

Again, the first thing Jesus said to Zacchaeus was 'Zacchaeus, be quick and come down; I must stay with you today', Luke tells us that Zacchaeus climbed down as fast as he could from the sycamore tree in which he was sitting and welcomed Jesus gladly. As in the case of the woman, there was surprise that Jesus had asked this favour. The eagerness of Zacchaeus suggests that this was the last thing he had expected. And among the crowd walking with Jesus there was a general murmur of disapproval as they said 'He has gone in to be the guest of a sinner' (Luke 19:1-10).

These incidents have two things in common.

First, both the woman at the well and the little man up the tree were, in some measure, outcasts of society. We have already mentioned them among the lonely, unwanted individuals about whom Jesus cared.

It is thought that the woman at the well had come in the heat of the noonday to draw water because she knew it was unlikely that at that hour she would encounter any of the other women, whose disapproval of the way she was living she dreaded to face.

Zacchaeus, too, probably felt himself to be an outsider. We wonder why he, as a top-ranking civil servant, needed to lose his dignity by climbing a tree to have a better view of Jesus. If he was a short man, we think, surely the crowds would have allowed him to go through to the front where he could see, especially considering his position as superintendent of taxes. But, though he had position and money, Zacchaeus was a member of an unpopular profession, and probably a particularly unpopular member at that, in view of his responsibility over other tax-gatherers and his reputation, judging from what he himself said later, of having enriched himself in dishonest ways. If, added to this, he had the feeling of inadequacy at times experienced by some of those who are short of stature, we can understand why he did not want to risk a snub by pushing through to the front of the crowd.

The other feature in common between these two incidents in which Jesus asked a favour is the surprise caused by his request. In neither instance was he asking a routine favour that might have been expected of Him. On both occasions He was making a request that struck at the roots of prejudice.

Both these features are worth careful thought on the part of those engaged in the Church's mission.

There are many lonely people in the world whose greatest need is to be of use to someone. They would echo John Wesley's prayer, 'Lord, let me not live to be useless'. Sometimes they are balked in their desire to be of use by people who like to be independent, who 'won't be beholden to anyone'. Such people do not know what a service they would be rendering to others if they made more use of them, consulted them more often, asked more often for their help.

The surprise caused by the fact that Jesus asked a favour of the Samaritan woman and of Zacchaeus is akin to the surprise we sometimes encounter when we ask help from someone who thinks he is of no use to anybody. Sometimes we encounter disapproval from others, as Jesus did from the crowd when He invited Himself to Zacchaeus's house. There were no doubt good-living people there who felt they should have been asked before this outsider. Sometimes, in the life of a Christian Church, the minister who draws in new people and tries to make them feel they belong by asking for their help in some activity finds there are others well established in the Church who feel that they should have been asked. The youth leader trying to integrate his young people may be up against the same problem.

While it is true, as we have said, that to ask a favour of people is often a way into their hearts and a service we can render them, it needs to be done prayerfully and wisely. Jesus did not ask favours of everybody, for this is not the way with some. There are people who have a suspicion that everyone wants to impose upon them and use them, and such people may prefer not to be asked. But in these days when there is so much service needed and so few Christians available to give it, we are more likely to make a mistake by not asking people for their help than by asking for it.

This was a lesson David Livingstone learned from experience. One day he was trying to make friends with Mpende, an African chief, who was suspicious of all white men, fearing that they might want to take his men as slaves. Then a message came from Livingstone, asking for the loan of a canoe to take a sick man across the river. At once the attitude of the African chief changed, and he warmed towards the missionary explorer. 'Only a true friend,' said Mpende, 'would ask me to help him.'

Jesus showed Himself a true friend to the woman at the well and to Zacchaeus. There are people today waiting for the same sign of friendship from the individual Christian and from the Church.

(g) He did not force Himself upon them

As we saw when we were considering the attitude of Jesus, He did not easily give up; but before we leave the subject of His approach to people we must notice that He did not force himself upon them.

In the temptations, Jesus rejected the way of approach that would have made it almost impossible for people not to believe in Him (Matthew 4 : 1-10). Faith is not faith if it is forced upon people, and one of the reasons why he deterred those He healed from telling of it (e.g. Mark 1:34; 5:43; 7:36) may have been because He did not want people's faith in Him to rest on miracles they had seen performed.

When Jesus sent the disciples out to preach, He told them to pass on from a town that did not receive them to another place (Luke 9:5; 10:10f.). In these passages about shaking the dust off their feet, He was clearly indicating to the Twelve and the Seventy that He did not want them to try to force their message upon unwilling hearers, but to give as many others as possible the chance to hear it.

In the incident when James and John wanted to call down fire from heaven to consume a village of the Samaritans that would not have Jesus because He was making for Jerusalem, it is clear that He did not feel the same resentment that some of His disciples felt when He was thus rejected. He did not knock again on this door that had been closed to Him, but led His disciples on to another village (Luke 9:51-56).

In Luke's Gospel this incident is immediately followed by an account of three potential disciples which makes the same point clear. The first of these volunteered to follow Jesus wherever he went, but Jesus reminded him that he might have to be homeless if he did become a disciple. The second was called by Jesus Himself, but asked to be excused until his father was dead and buried. The third offered to join the disciples, but wanted to say good-bye first to his people at home (Luke 9:57-62).

These verses make it plain that Jesus was not in any

way cheapening discipleship or touting for followers. In telling men that those who followed Him must deny themselves, take up their cross, and go where He went (Luke 9:23), He seemed almost to be trying to put people off. Certainly He was showing that He did not want to force Himself on anyone.

There is, of course, a certain tension between the point that we are making here and the point we made earlier that Jesus did not easily give up. Both can be substantiated from the Gospels, however, and both have their place in our thinking about mission.

The importance of not easily giving up in our Christian mission we have already emphasized. We need now to look at the implications for us of the fact that He did not force Himself on people.

It needs to be looked at first from the point of view of our theology. If we try to force the gospel down people's throats, we are implying two things: first, that more depends on our efforts and the pressure we put on people than depends on the work of the Spirit of God; second, that it is possible for us to decide that a person shall believe, so that his response to Jesus Christ is really our response forced upon him. The heart of evangelism is the spreading of the gospel, not the producing of results. If this were not so, some faithful missionary who may have offered the gospel in a Buddhist area for twenty years without seeing one conversion would not have been evangelizing. Our commission is to preach the gospel in word and service; only the Holy Spirit can regenerate a man, and only the man himself, and not the one who is trying to win him, can decide whether he is to respond to or to refuse the offer of Christ.

This matter needs to be looked at also from the point of view of our strategy. To attempt to bulldoze or brain-wash a person is not, in this modern world, calculated to win him. Rather it is calculated to alienate him. However immature people may often seem to be in their reactions, they like to be treated as responsible adults with a right to minds of their own. The whole outlook of Western man regarding communication and advertising has changed. No longer does the advertiser challenge or put the reader 'on the spot'. He allows the reader to retain his dignity and self-respect, and suggests to him in much subtler ways than before the point he is being asked to consider. Even the door-to-door salesman is trained not to force himself on anyone.

The world must not, of course, be allowed to dictate to the Church how it shall go to work. But the Church's mission must be presented in a way that does not gratu-itously run counter to the cultural environment in which it is being presented. And it does so run counter if we attempt to force ourselves or our gospel on those to whom we go as Christians.

Having stated the case for not trying to bully people into the Kingdom of God, we must be careful not to overstate it. We are not advocating a casual, take-it-or-leave-it presentation of Christian faith. If we are burn-ingly convinced, then burning conviction should show itself. We are not to pretend to be less keen than we are that people should become Christians. The New Testa-ment presentation of the gospel is described in language like this: Peter 'pressed his case and pleaded with them' (Acts 2 :40), and 'Saul grew more and more forceful, and silenced the Jews of Damascus with his cogent proofs that Jesus was the Messiah' (Acts 9:22). Christian mission is a matter of urgency, and it must be seen that we believe it to be so. All we are saying is that as we engage in it we must not fall into the trap of appearing to take everything upon ourselves, leaving nothing to the Holy Spirit. We are saying that we must respect the dignity of human personality and must not appear as a burglar breaking and entering the house of a man's life. Like Jesus, we shall not force ourselves or our message upon him.

THREE

The Method of Jesus

THE CHRISTIAN properly reacts against any suggestion that Jesus had a 'technique'. Rather, we may put it that there was a way he went to work as He engaged in the mission of God. And from that way, that method, the Christian has much to learn.

(a) He went and looked for men

As the Good Shepherd (John 10:11), Jesus was like the one of whom He told in the parable of the lost sheep, who was ready to leave the ninety-nine in the open pasture in order to go after the missing one, and who went on looking until he found it (Luke 15:4). He was sent to the lost sheep of the house of Israel (Matthew 15:24). He was sent by the Lord who says, 'Go out on to the highways and along the hedgerows and make them come in; I want my house to be full' (Luke 14:23).

Jesus did not have far to go to seek for people: there

were usually plenty of them seeking for Him, as we saw when we were considering how He spent Himself for others. But the very fact of His ministry in Galilee and Judaea was a sign that He was looking for men. John the Baptist had withdrawn from the towns and villages and had made for the wilderness, and the contacts we find John having with people were mostly in that setting. But Jesus made for where people were. He taught in their synagogues, sat in their homes, and talked in their streets. He had come for others and He made for where they were to be found.

Apart from this general picture, however, there are some particular occasions in the gospels where we are given glimpses of Him looking for men. We see it, for example, in the passage where the people of Capernaum pressed Him to remain with them, and He said, 'I must give the good news of the kingdom of God to the other towns also, for that is what I was sent to do' (Luke 4:42-44).

On the Mount of Transfiguration, Peter proposed that they should remain in that place where the glory of Jesus had been revealed to them and they had seen portrayed the law and the prophets' witness to Him in the persons of Moses and Elijah. But next day Jesus led the three disciples down the mountain to where people were and where need was waiting for Him in the form of an epileptic boy, his distraught father, and a group of powerless disciples (Luke 9:37-43).

We must not suppose that all the contacts of Jesus with tax-gatherers and sinners were random contacts with people He happened to meet. He knew He was called to help them, and we may take it that He sought them out. We have one instance of this in the story of Zacchaeus (Luke 19:1-10). Jesus had plenty to keep Him busy that day as He took His last journey to Jerusalem. The easier course for Him would have been to keep in the company of those who were walking on the road with Him and perhaps to slip quietly into the home of some good man who would have been glad to entertain Him. Instead, He actively sought out someone in greater need. He called up to Zacchaeus and asked if He might stay with him. Zacchaeus might have found his feet in his career, but as far as his knowledge of God and of goodness was concerned, he was lost. But to look for such people was just what Jesus had come for. As the Lord said at the end of that day: 'The Son of Man has come to seek and save what is lost.'

In these days people do not often come to seek us out and ask the way to God, though they often come with their reasons why they cannot believe in Him. When people do come, the Christian rejoices to try to help them. But we were never intended to wait until they came to us. We are called to the much harder task of going out and seeking them.

The essential note of the New Testament is 'Go' rather than 'Come'. It does not speak of indoor meetings to which people outside the Church are invited to come. It speaks rather of Christians going into all the world to preach the gospel.

For a long time the Christian Church in most countries has emphasised the 'Come' rather than the 'Go'. At its worst, the Church has not bothered much with either word and has been more like a club to which the members make their way for their own good. Most Churches have been better than that, however. They have at least had notices outside saying what was going on and inviting people in. This is good so far as it goes, but it does not correspond to the picture of the Church in New Testament times, or to the picture of Jesus the gospels give us.

Today, with the renewed interest there is in mission, the Church is waking up to the fact that it exists not for itself but for others, that mission carries the meaning of being sent, and that if we are sent it means we have to go!

Think of a political party at election time. If in any constituency a party decided to do nothing but hold an indoor meeting in any town it could, that party would almost certainly not win the election. It knows that if it held indoor meetings, not more than a few would attend, and that the way to get somewhere is to go out where people are, out to the farms and the houses and the factory gates.

Christians are often slow to recognize that if a political candidate goes out where people are, while the Church in its mission stays within four walls, the implication to the world is plain: that what the Church has to offer is much less important than what the political party has to offer.

The question remains: for what purpose is the Church to go out and look for men? Two answers tend to be given, according to the viewpoint held.

Over-simplifying a little, one may say that the evangelical tends to think of mission almost exclusively in terms of evangelism. We are to go out and look for men with the direct and avowed objective of making Jesus

Christ known. We shall be out on the streets, or visiting people's homes, or mixing in the community, with one hope above others in our mind: that men and women may be converted.

At the other extreme, many radicals assert that conversion is unnecessary, that evangelism smacks too much of proselytism, and that what the Christian is to do in the world is to provide a Christian presence, to sit where men sit, to serve and help where he can, but not to pretend that he knows many answers, and not to presume to verbalize his faith.

This dichotomy between evangelism and service is alien to the spirit of Jesus. Jesus went out and looked for men, and sent the Twelve and the Seventy out, with a comprehensive ministry, a ministry that included evangelism and service, preaching the gospel on the one hand and offering healing and help on the other.

What God has joined together we have no authority for putting asunder. There are some encouraging signs that we are learning from one another. In the current debate on the mission of the Church we are learning to think of it primarily as God's mission entrusted to His people, and gradually we are coming to see the breadth of that mission.

On the one hand, many evangelicals are less inclined than formerly to consider social action as a sphere to be left to the politicians and to think that nothing matters but evangelism. Remembering the contribution made to social progress by the early evangelicals of the eighteenth and nineteenth centuries,[1] and recognizing that an emphasis on the service aspect of mission does not

[1] See, e.g., Kathleen Heasman, *Evangelicals in Action*, Bles.

63

necessarily involve replacing a spiritual by a social gospel, they are coming to see that looking for men that we may share our faith with them in no way excludes looking for men that we may serve them.

At the same time, some radicals at least are more ready than they were to recognize that there is a place for evangelism as well as service. Though they may disapprove, as indeed some evangelicals would do, of some past and present methods of evangelism, and though what they mean by the gospel may be very different in detail from what the evangelical means,[1] they are coming to see that men need to be confronted with the offer of Jesus Christ, that this can best be done face to face, that there is a proper place for verbalizing our testimony, and that to have some share in this is the privilege of the rank-and-file Christian and not only of the specialist.

As was said in the Introduction to this book, mission is all that God sent us out to do. This includes the spreading of His gospel and the serving of all men in their need. It is not either evangelism or service, according to taste. It is both evangelism and service, in obedience to our orders. And, like Jesus, to do both we need to go out and look for men.

(b) He sometimes dealt with two people together

In John 1:35-39 we see Jesus meeting and spending the rest of the day with two prospective disciples, Andrew and, probably, John. In the next verses we see

[1] For a useful discussion of this from the evangelical point of view, see the Report of the Evangelical Alliance Commission on Evangelism, *On the Other Side*, pp. 67f., 83-87.

Him with Andrew and Simon Peter, and then with another couple, Philip and Nathanael (John 1 : 40-49).

This seems to have been a first meeting with the five we have mentioned, and earlier than the call of the first disciples described in the other Gospels. Here also, however, Jesus called them in pairs: first Simon and Andrew, and then James and John (Mark 1 : 16-20).

Matthew tells us of an occasion when two blind men followed Jesus and asked for healing. After Jesus had restored their sight He asked them not to make it known, but the pair of them spread it all over the countryside (Matthew 9 : 27-31).

On the evening of the first Easter Day it was to two on the road to Emmaus that Jesus appeared. He led them through to belief in His resurrection and then, in their home, was made known to them in the breaking of bread (Luke 24 : 13-35).

We draw attention to this feature of Jesus' ministry because sometimes those most actively concerned with mission have neglected the opportunity of dealing with people in pairs. Those engaged in personal evangelism have often felt that it was necessary to arrange to see people on their own before any progress could be made in leading them to Christian faith.

The way Jesus approached pairs of people, however, draws our attention to the fact that sometimes it is the most natural thing for a pair of friends to hear the gospel together and together to put their trust in Christ as Saviour and Friend. If two people are bound up in the bundle of life together, two friends, or brothers, or sisters, or a husband and wife, or boy-friend and girl-friend, they will be used to doing things together, and

65

either may hesitate to take such a vital step as commit-
ting himself to Christ in the absence of the other. Each
must make a personal response, of course, but they can
often be led to it unitedly. Then, when both have
started together on the Christian way, they can stand by
one another in a way that will be the greatest strength
to both.

(c) He knew the value of eating with men

The Fourth Gospel tells us that the first sign that led the
disciples to believe in Him was Jesus' turning the water
into wine at a wedding feast at Cana in Galilee (John
2:1-11).

In spite of the prejudice it aroused, Jesus persisted in
eating with the tax-gatherers and sinners. When, after
he had responded to the call to be a disciple, Levi held a
big reception in his house for Jesus, among the guests was
a large party of tax-gatherers and others. It was when
the Pharisees and lawyers complained about His eating
with such company that Jesus said it was not the healthy
that needed the doctor, but the sick (Luke 5:29-32).
Later, in Luke 15:2, the complaint is renewed: 'This
fellow welcomes sinners and eats with them.'

Jesus was not put off by these criticisms, and right at
the end of His ministry he still faced the same objection,
'He has gone in to be the guest of a sinner', when He
went to spend the day in the house of Zacchaeus. This
incident gives us an idea of what Jesus was able to
achieve as He sat eating with these men whom others
condemned and left alone. At the end of that day,
Zacchaeus seemed a new man, no longer concerned
with feathering his own nest, but clear in his mind as to

66

how much he was going to give to charity and how many times over he was going to repay any whom he had cheated in the past (Luke 19:1-10).

Jesus' liking for sharing meals with others was evidently well known and was twisted by His enemies into a reputation for being a glutton and drinker (Luke 7:34). This accusation was made particularly in the context of His sharing meals with the tax-gatherers and sinners. But these were not the only ones outside the circle of His immediate friends with whom He was happy to share a meal. In the incident that in Luke's Gospel immediately follows, Jesus was invited to a meal in the house of a Pharisee named Simon. In spite of the fact that Simon seems to have asked Him in order to look Him up and down and to decide whether or not He was a true prophet, and in spite of the fact that Simon had omitted the common courtesies in those days of providing Him, on his arrival, with water to wash His feet, of giving Him a kiss of welcome, and of offering Him oil for his hair as He came in from the hot sun, Jesus accepted the hospitality of that home and took His place at table (Luke 7:36-50).

The Gospels give us occasional glimpses of His eating in the homes of those who believed in Him, such as the home at Bethany, where Martha complained because Mary was not lending her a hand (Luke 10:38-42). Some think that when Jesus said, 'Martha, Martha, you are fretting and fussing about so many things; but one thing is necessary', He was suggesting that a simple meal of one dish was all He needed. It was not the elaborate provision of many dishes that attracted Him to people's homes; it was the opportunity of sitting with them and eating with them.

The most unusual setting in which Jesus is seen eating with men is provided by the incidents of the feeding of the five thousand and of the four thousand (Mark 6:32-44; 8:1-10). Here were common meals with Jesus that none who were present could ever forget.

In view of the place that eating with men took in the story of Jesus, it is not surprising that on the eve of His death He chose the setting of a meal for His last conversation with His disciples, and that the way of remembering Him that He chose for them was in the breaking of bread and the drinking of wine, as at that last supper (Matthew 26:26-29; I Corinthians 11:23-26).

After the resurrection, there are several incidents in which Jesus is reported to have eaten with His disciples and others. He is invited into the home at Emmaus of the two who have been walking the seven miles from Jerusalem in His company. There, as He takes bread, says the blessing, breaks the bread, and offers it to them, their eyes are opened and they recognize who He is (Luke 24:28-31). The same evening, back at Jerusalem, the two from Emmaus are telling their story to the other disciples when, as they are talking, there Jesus is, standing among them. Luke records that Jesus asks them, 'Have you anything here to eat?' When they offer Him a piece of fish they have cooked, He takes it and eats before their eyes (Luke 24:33-43).

The last meal the Gospels record Jesus as enjoying with His disciples take place during the period after the resurrection when seven of the disciples have been out fishing on the Sea of Tiberias. After Jesus, standing on the shore, has called to tell them where to put their net, and they have come ashore dragging the net full of big fish, Jesus says to them, 'Come and have breakfast.' While they have been bringing their boat to shore, Jesus has been cooking breakfast for them over a charcoal fire. So the Risen Lord waits on them once more, distributing bread and fish to them all, as they picnic together beside the sea (John 21:1-13).

Our thoughts about the implications of all this for the mission of the Church will naturally begin with the Lord's Supper. With the exception of the Society of Friends and the Salvation Army, practically the whole Christian Church is united in agreeing that Jesus intended the Church to continue to do in remembrance of Him what He did at the last supper in taking the bread and wine and sharing it with His disciples.

The frequency with which this is done varies tremendously from one tradition to another, ranging from a quarterly to a daily communion. There is also an enormous variation in the meaning implied, the language used, the simplicity or elaborateness of the ritual, the kinds of bread and wine used, and the physical arrangements made for receiving these. Sadly, it must be added that the differences are so great that Christians of some churches are debarred from receiving holy communion in the churches of some other denominations, so that a sacrament that so finely symbolizes unity and the sharing of a common life has come to be a symbol of disunity.

To this unhappy situation those concerned with Christian unity are now addressing themselves. Churches of varying traditions are learning from one another, and the differences between modes of celebration are less marked than they were. Thinking of the matter, as we are doing here, in a setting of Christian mission, the following hopes may be expressed to those in a position to influence the shape of our communion services in all denominations.

First, the more we can move towards a common practice the better the cause of mission will be served, as those of one tradition will then be the better able to receive the gospel in the sacrament in a church of another tradition with a feeling of being at home.

Second, the remaining considerable problems in the way of inter-communion must be tackled resolutely, and we must take seriously the motivation for unity that Jesus stated: 'that the world may believe' (John 17:21f.).

Third, while holy communion is primarily for the fellowship of believers with their Lord, the service can be, and has been for many, as John Wesley said, 'a converting ordinance'; and any modification of the order of service must ensure that the gospel is preached in word as well as in act, and that it can still be said that in this service we are proclaiming the death of the Lord until He comes (I Corinthians 11:26).

Fourth, for this service to play its part in Christian mission, the language must be simple and intelligible. The Lord's Supper is no place for esoteric allusions, comprehensible only to the initiated. This does not mean that theological language must be absent, but that everything possible should be done to ensure that what the service is communicating shall be communicated in a way that has meaning for the simple as well as the intelligent.

Fifth, the changes that are being made in the actions that are performed in the communion service should also be made in the direction of simplicity, as is indeed happening at the present time. If the holy communion is to play its part in mission, there is as little place for esoteric action as for esoteric language. Furthermore, if the fact that this is a re-enactment of the Last Supper, which was a common meal in the simple setting of the Upper Room, is to be kept before the communicant, the simpler the service the better it will be.

Finally, in the arrangement of the church and the arrangements that are made for communicants to receive the elements, it will help demonstrate the reality of what is being done if, as nearly as circumstances allow, what is done resembles the partaking of a common meal together. For this reason current trends towards having a communion table among the people, with the presiding minister behind it, may be welcomed.

The implications for mission of the fact that Jesus knew the value of eating with men go far beyond the question of the Lord's Supper, however.

The early Church appears to have had a common meal, which we know as the *Agape,* and a number of attempts have been made to provide something analogous to it in the Church of later centuries. The early Methodists had a love-feast at which water and a little plain cake were taken and testimonies were given to the Christian experience of those present. A very few of these love-feasts still continue.

I remember in my 'teens attending what was called an

Agape in a Baptist Church in Paris. We all sat round a table, drank chocolate and conversed together, and the pastor's little daughter stood on a form and gave a recitation.

To attempt to re-create the *Agape* today would probably seem artificial, and people would only be self-conscious. The modern counterpart might well be something much more like the church picnic that we have seen in the United States on a Sunday evening, followed by fellowship together, or the Church Supper Club, with a talk and questions after the tables have been cleared. The Youth Camp sing-song, testimonies, and talk over the supper tables, and even the C.S.S.M. camp fire sausage sizzle and talk, may have something to contribute to a model for this. What is needed is not an artificially contrived, stilted occasion, where people feel uneasy because of the unfamiliarity and are not quite sure whether to be as silent and solemn as they would be at a communion service. Rather, the atmosphere needed is that of a family party: the church family eating out together, enjoying, not a token meal, but the food they like to eat, and enjoying one another's company also. Relaxed informality, no embargo on humour, a sense of occasion, a reminder of the fact that Jesus Christ is there in the midst, an opportunity for some spontaneous sharing of what God has done for us, these are the things that can contribute towards giving such an evening a little of the character of the reception Matthew gave in honour of Jesus and to introduce his friends to the Lord. We tell people that the Church is a family, and we need, if our mission is to be effective, more occasions when it can be seen to be one.

Remembering that mission takes in service as well as evangelism, the church 'At Home' can sometimes serve the cause of mission in this wider sense. The average church often leaves to the city mission the provision of parties for old people and such things as Christmas dinners for the lonely. The servant role of the Church would be more clearly seen and recognized if, for example, a church were sometimes at home to residents of the nearest Old People's Home, or if the local club for the disabled sometimes received an invitation to an evening with the church people, both with transport provided.

(d) He knew the value of using the home

Most of the occasions when Jesus ate with his friends or with the tax-gatherers and others were in the setting of an ordinary meal in an ordinary home. He knew the value of using the home as much as He knew the value of eating with men, and the two generally went together. This, too, has its importance for mission.

The New Testament commends the practice of hospitality (Romans 12:13; I Timothy 3:2; Titus 1:8; Hebrews 13:2; I Peter 4:9), and it has always been regarded as a Christian responsibility. It has its place in both the evangelism and the service aspects of mission.

Jesus' use of homes to further His mission began when John the Baptist's two disciples were walking behind Him one day. He turned to speak to them, saying, 'What are you looking for?' When they asked where He was staying, instead of merely telling them, He said, 'Come and see.' They went and saw where he was staying, and spent the rest of the day with Him (John 1:37-39). So the two were helped in the direction of discipleship by a home being opened to them that day.

From that time on, in the passages we discussed where He is seen eating with men, and in others as well, Jesus is seen in and out of homes, sometimes giving, and more often receiving, hospitality. In these opened homes, at table and at other times, His mission was being fulfilled. The sick were healed, the gospel was preached, men's questions were answered, the seeking were counselled in these homes that someone had put at His disposal. There must have been times when His hosts were greatly inconvenienced through no fault of Jesus, as when the roof of a house was opened up by the four who brought the paralytic to Jesus (Mark 2 : 1-4). But homes were opened up to Him all over the country, and, in these homes, the work of His mission went on.

The importance of all this today is being seen with increasing clarity. As far as the evangelism side of mission is concerned, the house group is proving increasingly valuable, as many people, more conscious than ever of a gulf between them and the Church, are often prepared to come to coffee in a neighbour's home and hear what a representative of the Church has to say. As far as the service side of mission is concerned, the frequent movement of population, and the increasing number of young people going away from home for education and training and of students from overseas coming to our country, make the service of Christian hospitality more needful than ever.

One final aspect of this must be mentioned. All engaged in evangelism know from experience what a vital part the opened home has to play in helping young people who want to become Christians. It is probably true that every adolescent needs a home other than the home of his parents into which he can go to talk things over. This is particularly true of the boy or girl from a non-Christian home who is coming into the life of the Church or who is accepting Christ as His Lord and Saviour. Our experience is that the answer to the question whether such a teenager will keep on the Christian road or be sucked back again into the world of unbelief depends more on the availability of an opened Christian home than on any other factor. The young Christian greatly needs someone to go to at any time with his problems and difficulties, with his doubts and his questions, and many Christian couples perform a service of this kind at great cost to themselves. They keep open house to young people who often do not know how to behave, have little idea when it is suitable to call and to leave, and make great inroads into the Christian couple's privacy. But for the sake of the mission of Jesus, the home stays open.

The early Church met in people's homes, and many of the local churches known to us did the same until larger numbers necessitated the building of separate places for worship. Experience on new housing estates has often shown that, while something has been gained, something has also been lost when the house church has given way to the church in a special building. Perhaps God wants us to rediscover in our generation what Jesus knew so well: the value of using a home in Christian mission.

(e) He spent much time training others

Jesus was able to command the attention of multitudes

who at times crowded from great distances to hear Him and watch Him heal the sick. But, though He gave them the attention and care, the teaching and healing they wanted, the top priority for Him clearly seems to have been the training of the few.

Under other headings we have already noticed the passage in John 1:35-51 in which Jesus takes time and trouble meeting and getting to know Andrew, Peter, Philip, Nathanael, and another, probably John. We have reminded ourselves of the scene by the lake where the first four disciples are called from their fishing (Mark 1:16-20) and of the call of Matthew from his custom-house (Matthew 9:9).

The full list of the twelve disciples is given in Mark 3:13-19 and parallel passages. Luke 6:12 says that the appointment of the Twelve followed a whole night of prayer by Jesus. This decision was clearly of the greatest possible importance to Him.

The list of names includes some of whom we know much in the rest of the New Testament and some of whom we know next to nothing. They varied in background, in the careers they had followed, and in natural gifts. One was to prove a traitor.

Mark introduces them with the words, 'He appointed twelve as his companions, whom he would send out to proclaim the Gospel, with a commission to drive out devils' (Mark 3:14). The Authorised Version says very simply in verse 14, 'He ordained twelve, that they should be with him, and that he might send them forth to preach.' Their being with Him was their discipleship, for a disciple is a learner; their being sent forth to preach was their apostleship, for an apostle is one sent out.

Most of the gospel story has to do with the first of these two things: their discipleship. As the story of Jesus unfolds, we find Him spending a great deal of time with these twelve men whom He was training.

Occasionally we read of His talking with an individual disciple, such as Peter (e.g. Luke 22:31-34), Andrew (John 6:8-10), Philip (John 14:8f.), and the other Judas, not Iscariot (John 14:22). Sometimes two of them together are speaking with Him, for example James and John (Mark 10:35-40) and Philip and Andrew (John 12:20-22). On several occasions the three who seem to have been closest to Him, Peter, James, and John, were in His company when others were not, as at the raising of Jairus's daughter (Luke 8:51), on the Mount of Transfiguration (Luke 9:28), and in the Garden of Gethsemane (Mark 14:33).

Mostly, however, it is the disciples in general who are referred to, as they join Him at a wedding feast (John 2:1-11), walk with Him through the cornfields (Mark 2:23), row Him across the sea (e.g. Mark 4:35-41), or talk over their problems with Him in the home (e.g. Mark 9:28).

But they were to be with Him that he might send them forth, and the Gospels tell of two preaching and healing tours in which they took part. The sending out of the Twelve is described in Luke 9:1-6 and the sending out of the Seventy in Luke 10:1-20. In addition to these preaching tours, they were, of course, also being trained for their ultimate responsibility to preach the gospel and serve men for Christ's sake after Jesus' visible presence had been withdrawn from them and they were out on their own. We can imagine that Peter and others in the days of the Acts of the Apostles were thankful for the training and experience that they had been given during the Lord's earthly ministry.

The detailed instructions given to those whom Jesus sent out may have been for that time and for their special situation rather than of permanent application, but there are a number of things in the fact and nature of the training Jesus gave the disciples that are of great relevance for the Church's mission today.

First, the time Jesus gave to training is important. The fact that at times He deliberately seemed to try to avoid the crowds to have time alone with the disciples indicates the value He attached to this part of His work. Ministers today have to make many difficult decisions with regard to the apportioning of their time. Many feel that training others should have higher priority than it has been given in the past. It is increasingly being recognized that the ministry is the ministry of the whole Church and that, as is said in Ephesians 4:11f., the gifts given to pastors and teachers are to equip God's people for work in His service.

Second, there is a sense in which what Jesus did was both ministerial training and lay training. Those who were to assume main responsibility in His Church as full-time leaders were given about three years of training by Jesus. But there were evidently others who were included in the Seventy and who, we must assume, had not had the privilege of being itinerant disciples of Jesus for anything like the time that the Twelve had had. But they had received enough training to be given responsibility and to be entrusted with His gospel. This also the Church today seems to be recognizing more and more. Lay training is playing an important part in the programme of all the Churches, and the Churches are considering in what ways the service for which laymen are to be trained is different from the service for which those to be ordained are trained.

A third feature of the training Jesus gave is its variety and informality. He did not give them neatly-wrapped parcels of doctrine. Rather He had them thinking for themselves on the basis of the hints and pointers He had given them. He often did not give a full explanation until they asked Him for it. In other words, He took them only as fast and as far as they were capable of going. They were learning by living with Him and by watching Him.

The structured form of college training as it has developed in the last 150 years is perhaps inevitable, but it is interesting to notice that some of the features of the training that Jesus gave are being considered in changes taking place in adult education, where people are encouraged to think and find things out for themselves, and where questions and discussion and programming to fit the individual's pace of development all have their part to play. The Church, in its training of people for mission, might long ago have learned some of these things from Jesus.

A fourth feature to notice is the fact that Jesus did not stay with them all the time, but prepared them for being out on their own. This is particularly true of the times they spent on their preaching and healing tours, but there were other times also, as when Jesus and three of the disciples were on the Mount of Transfiguration and the rest were on their own, trying to cope with the epileptic boy who had been brought to them for healing (Luke 9 : 37-43).

We learn by doing, and an indispensable part of training is doing. Any apprentice will learn first by watching and being told, and then by being given the opportunity of doing himself what he has seen and heard about. We who are in the ministry are sometimes unduly timid about thrusting people out into the world to engage in mission. Jesus, in one sense, took a calculated risk, especially when He sent out the Seventy, some of whom must have had less training than the Twelve; but the risk was justified, and they returned to report that God had used them beyond their expectations (Luke 10 : 17).

Finally, Jesus' use of the team method and of pairs of disciples is worth noticing. It must have been a strength to each one of the Twelve and of the Seventy to know that the others were in action at the same time and probably facing the same needs and difficulties that they were. By sending them in a team, Jesus was sending them with the feeling of being a force that God could use. But by dividing them up into pairs rather than sending large numbers together, he was spreading the blessing they took with them more widely than would otherwise have been possible.

We may wonder why He did not spread it even more widely by sending them out as individuals. He knew human nature enough to know that it needs the moral support that one of a pair of people can give the other. He knew also how often the gifts of two people are complementary to one another, and that the personality of one would carry conviction to some of those to whom they went and the personality of the other to others. And while they were inexperienced, being in a pair would give each of them at every point a colleague to consult. There was also the added impact of a second voice. The Jewish law required that in a charge against anyone two or three witnesses were required (Deuteronomy 19:15). In the preaching of the gospel Jesus was sending out a pair of witnesses to corroborate one another's testimony.

Many engaged in mission today have proved the value both of team witness and of sending people out in pairs. This can be of value in the service aspect as well as in the evangelism aspect of mission. The inspired methods of Jesus so long ago have proved here, as in so many other ways, to be timeless in their application.[1]

(f) *He knew that teaching method mattered*

Those who wish to communicate anything important, and in particular those who have a share in the mission of God, have much to learn from the teaching methods of Jesus. The subject is worth a longer study than is possible here, but some points at least can be made.

1. The teaching of Jesus was *simple* yet *profound*. Its homeliest references and easiest words open up the great mysteries of God and man, yet Jesus did not go in for long abstruse discussions nor did he deal much in the abstract. He gave men simple statements, with great economy of words. The Aramaic language helped, for it had simple and colourful ways of saying things.

[1] For a much fuller treatment of the training methods of Jesus, see Fred Milson, *His Leadership and Ours,* Epworth Press.

Yet the implications of the sayings of Jesus are inexhaustible and give rise to an almost endless train of thought. Who will ever fathom the I AM sayings of the Fourth Gospel or plumb the depths of the parables?

2. The teaching of Jesus *began with experience*. It was linked at every point with familiar life, the life of the shepherd, farmer, fisherman, housewife, or child. Everyday things such as money and animals were his texts. The fact that the teaching of Jesus was remembered in such detail during the many years when it circulated as oral tradition shows how vivid it was to those who heard it.

3. The teaching of Jesus was *arresting*. It was challenging and always thought-provoking. It was often startling and paradoxical. It sometimes angered people and always made them curious, and so challenged them to think. His teaching was never dull. No one can have been bored when he was speaking in such paradoxes as 'He that saves his life shall lose it', and 'The first shall be last', or making startling statements like those about going the second mile and turning the other cheek.

4. The teaching of Jesus was *emphatic*. His was not the mild, casual, take-it-or-leave-it teaching that finishes up 'So we see that there is much to be said on both sides'. His 'Verily, verily' (Greek : 'Amen, amen'), his use of repetition, 'Again I say to you', his sets of parables all pointing in the same direction, show that He knew the value of giving more than one tap with the hammer.

5. The teaching of Jesus made use of the *question method*. We have seen earlier how seriously He took the questions others asked Him. He, too, often asked questions of those He taught. He involved his listeners in

what was being said and done, as we are learning today to involve those who are being taught in a way in which they were not previously involved in the learning process.

The Christian engaged in mission needs, then, to remember that it is not only what we say, but how we say it, that matters. Christians need to study all the new insights into teaching method and to use them in the task of mission, not only among children, but for all ages.

(g) *He spoke to men from Scripture*

The words of Scripture were often on the lips of Jesus, and he often made use of the Old Testament as he taught people about Himself and the eternal and abundant life He came to bring.

At the beginning of His ministry, in the synagogue at Nazareth, He reads from Isaiah 61, then tells them that in their very hearing that text has come true (Luke 4:16-21).

Among other passages He quoted are the words of Psalm 118:22f., saying to His hearers, Matthew tells us, 'Have you never read in the scriptures: "The stone which the builders rejected has become the main cornerstone. This is the Lord's doing, and it is wonderful in our eyes"?' (Matthew 21:42).

There are many other references to the Old Testament, especially in Matthew's Gospel, but the most memorable chapter from this point of view is Luke 24, which describes the first Easter Day. To the disillusioned pair walking to Emmaus He 'began with Moses and all the prophets, and explained to them the passages which referred to himself in every part of the scriptures'. Afterwards they said to one another that they had felt their hearts on fire as He talked to them on the road and explained the Scriptures to them (Luke 24:27,32).

Later the same evening, He was with the disciples at Jerusalem and, Luke tells us, said to them, 'This is what I meant by saying, while I was still with you, that everything written about me in the Law of Moses and in the prophets and psalms was bound to be fulfilled'. Then he opened their minds to understand the Scriptures and went on to speak in particular of the passages that foreshadowed the death and resurrection of the Messiah (Luke 24:44-47).

Jesus always spoke with respect of the Old Testament Scriptures. He had come not to abolish, but to complete the Law and the prophets (Matthew 5:17); the testimony of the Scriptures pointed to Him (John 5:39f.).

The fact that the Scriptures played so large a part in the teaching of Jesus does not mean that in our carrying out of His mission we should do little except quote from the Bible, for Jesus Himself more often taught in other ways and, in any case, those to whom we speak do not know their Bibles or accept their authority as did those to whom the Lord spoke. But these differences in our position have often been overstated. Although people do not know their Bibles as well as they did, we can still use them in evangelism, though we need to begin, as it were, further back in our explanation of what the Scriptures are saying. Although people do not so readily accept the authority of the Bible, they will often take more notice of what can be shown to be the teaching of Scripture than of something that appears to them the uncorroborated theory of ourselves as private individuals.

Some of us remember the first large crusade conducted by Billy Graham at Harringay, London, in 1954. People had been saying that Bible preaching would cut no ice in the 1950s, since people neither knew nor accepted the authority of the Bible. Then Billy Graham came, speaking always with his open Bible in his hand and reiterating 'the Bible says', 'the Bible says'; and the crowds came night after night and listened and responded. The press was intrigued, and many theories were produced to explain the impact of the evangelist's preaching. But one thing at least was inescapable: the words of Scripture were going home. As a reporter from one London daily described it: 'The hearer wilts before the merciless impact of the Good Book.' Those who had been so sure it was no good quoting the Bible to modern man were made to think again.

Those who have any doubt about the importance of the right use of Scripture in mission should read A. M. Chirgwin's book *The Bible in World Evangelism*[1] which tells remarkable stories of what the Scriptures have done, often without human comment, in awakening men to their need of God and showing them the way to find Him in Jesus Christ. The one engaged in the mission of God still needs the Scriptures. He will test his message by the yardstick of Bible doctrine; he will try to convey its message in words that modern man can understand; he will try to make sure that those he wins rest on the promises of God rather than on emotion; and he will encourage them to go forward seeking a

[1] S.C.M. Press.

word from the Lord in their own daily reading of the Bible. Like Jesus Himself, he will often have the words of Scripture on his lips.

(h) He confronted them with an either/or

We live in an age that does not care to see things in black and white. Tolerance has come to be exalted as almost the highest of all virtues. Truth and moral standards alike are thought of as relative rather than absolute.

To people living in this atmosphere it comes as something of a shock to face the clear-cut teaching of Jesus. We are accustomed to thinking in terms of for, against, and neutral; but there seems no room for neutrality as far as Jesus is concerned.

'He who is not with me is against me, and he who does not gather with me scatters,' He says on one occasion (Matthew 12 : 30); and on another, 'He who is not against us is on our side' (Mark 9 : 40). There is no neutrality there.

So it is also with His teaching. There is a wide road that leads to perdition and there is a narrow road that leads to life, but there is no mention of a middle way between the two (Matthew 7 : 13f.). There are good trees yielding good fruit and poor trees yielding bad fruit, and we are left to choose between them, with no further option of being a mediocre tree in between (Matthew 7 : 16-20). There is a house built on the rock and there is a house built on the sand; one stands and the other falls, and a man's acting or failing to act upon what Jesus says determines which of the two houses represents his life. There is again no middle way suggested (Matthew 7 : 24-27).

So we could go on, illustrating the either/or with which Jesus confronted men with such passages as the parables of the wheat and the darnel (Matthew 13:24-30), the good and the bad fish (Matthew 13:47-50), the rich man and Lazarus (Luke 16: 19-31), or the Pharisee and the tax-gatherer (Luke 18:9-14).

Jesus thought clearly and set issues clearly before men, especially the basic issue of a man or woman's relationship to God. Although it is always more difficult and more unpopular to point up issues in the way He did, He was faithful in His dealings with men, whatever the consequences.

Those engaged in the mission of Jesus must often make themselves face up to the same issue. It is easy to prune our gospel to match the mood of the day and to play down the sharp distinctions Jesus made. But there are some of us who have reason to be glad that there were those who were willing, when we were young, to confront us with an either/or that led us to face up to the offer and challenge of God in Christ. My own mind goes back to the C.S.S.M. workers at Weymouth who clarified the gospel for me, and to the Rev. W. J. Graham Hobson who clinched matters when he spoke about the one who said 'No' to Jesus and went on his way sorrowing (the Rich Young Ruler of Mark 10:17-22) and the one who said 'Yes' to Jesus and went on his way rejoicing (the Ethiopian eunuch of Acts 8:26-40). As a schoolboy I saw clearly at last the response I needed to make, and conscious Christian commitment began for me that day. Now I know that, however much easier it would be to dodge the issue, I too must help men and women to face the either/or with which Jesus confronts them.

(i) He led them to definite faith in Himself

The first three Gospels indicate that Jesus did not, at any rate at first, want it to be known that He was the Messiah. Thus, for example, Luke tells us of the day when the crowds gathered for healing at Capernaum and devils came out of many of them, shouting 'You are the Son of God', but He rebuked them and forbade them to speak, because they knew that He was the Messiah (Luke 4 :40f.).

When the disciples had come to see who He was, however, and Peter made his great confession of faith at Caesarea Philippi with the words, 'You are the Messiah, the Son of the Living God', Jesus said, 'Simon son of Jonah, you are favoured indeed! You did not learn that from mortal man; it was revealed to you by my heavenly Father' (Matthew 16 : 13-18).

From then on, the Messiahship of Jesus was a secret between His disciples and Himself, a secret the full meaning of which did not penetrate even their minds until after the resurrection. We have the impression, at least in the first three Gospels, that Jesus did not take active steps to lead others to assert that He was the Messiah; but he certainly led them towards faith in Him as one who could forgive sins.

The first occasion on which this occurs is when He speaks the words 'Your sins are forgiven' to the paralytic lowered through the roof into the room where He is teaching. He goes on to ask whether it is easier to say 'Your sins are forgiven' or to say 'Stand up and walk'.

But, to convince them that the Son of Man has the right on earth to forgive sins, He tells the paralytic to stand up, take his bed, and go home (Matthew 9:2-6).

Jesus makes the same public announcement of forgiveness to the sinful woman in the house of Simon the Pharisee. As in the story of the paralytic, when the Lord says to the woman, 'Your sins are forgiven', the others present begin to ask themselves, 'Who is this, that He can forgive sins?' Jesus then goes on to add these important words as He addresses the woman: 'Your faith has saved you; go in peace' (Luke 7:48-50). The woman has been saved, rescued, from her sins, not by her good resolutions, nor by her love, but by her faith, faith that she placed in Jesus Himself. The implications were there for all who heard to understand.

In the Fourth Gospel, there are more instances of Jesus' leading people to definite faith in Himself.

In John 1:43-51, Jesus draws out from Nathanael the confession 'You are the Son of God; you are king of Israel'.

In John 4:25f., Jesus shares the secret of His messiahship with the woman at the well, saying to her when she has referred to the coming Messiah, 'I am he, I who am speaking to you now'.

Later, in reply to the question 'What must we do if we are to work as God would have us work?' He replies, 'This is the work that God requires: believe in the one whom he has sent' (John 6:28f.).

Similarly, when Jesus hears that the man born blind whom He has cured has been expelled from the synagogue, He seeks him out and says, 'Have you faith in the Son of Man?' When the man asks who the Son of Man is that he should put his faith in Him, Jesus replies, 'You have seen him; indeed, it is he who is speaking to you'. 'Lord, I believe,' the man says, and bows before Him (John 9 : 34-38).

In the story of Lazarus, after saying that He is the resurrection and that He is life, and speaking about the life to which men come when they believe in Him, Jesus asks Martha, 'Do you believe this?' He wins from her a wonderful confession of faith: 'Lord, I do; I now believe that you are the Messiah, the Son of God who was to come into the world' (John 11 : 25-27).

To Thomas, after the resurrection, Jesus says, 'Be unbelieving no longer, but believe', and leads Thomas to say, 'My Lord and my God!' On hearing this great confession of faith from the man we call Doubting Thomas, Jesus says, 'Because you have seen me you have found faith. Happy are they who never saw me and yet have found faith' (John 20 : 27-29).

It was a part of the mission of Jesus to let Himself be revealed, at the right time and in the right way, as Son of Man, Messiah or Christ, and Son of God. All three titles are worthy of more detailed study than we can give them here.

The title Son of Man was not, as many people imagine, one that suggested mainly the humanity of Jesus. Sometimes it is used in a setting of His humiliation, as in Mark 8 : 31 ('He began to teach them that the Son of Man had to undergo great sufferings . . .'), and sometimes in a setting of His glory, as in Mark 14 : 62 ('You will see the Son of Man seated on the right hand of God and coming with the clouds of heaven'). From its

Old Testament background it carried associations of a representative man, of one receiving a kingdom, and of one coming with the clouds. It is the title Jesus used of Himself when making His most superhuman claims. In Him the title Son of Man seems for the first time to be linked with the Suffering Servant of Isaiah.

The title Messiah, or Christ, was a title others gave Jesus more than He gave it to Himself. It means 'Anointed One' and was, of course, the title the Jews gave to the coming king they expected from the line of David, in fulfilment of Old Testament prophecy. Jesus' most open public admission to being the Messiah is made to the High Priest in Mark 14:61f.

The title Son of God goes further than the title Messiah. The Gospels tell us that at the baptism of Jesus a voice from heaven was heard, saying, 'This is my Son, my Beloved, on whom my favour rests' (Matthew 3:17). Again, at the Transfiguration, we are told a voice called from the cloud, 'This is my Son, my Beloved, on whom my favour rests; listen to him' (Matthew 17:5), and in the Fourth Gospel He is reported as referring to Himself as God's son (Matthew 11:25-27).

We have gone in some detail into the ways in which Jesus led men to definite faith in Himself because of its importance for our own mission. Here is the heart of what the Christian has to proclaim. He has more to do than merely to talk about the love of God, or to commend the moral teaching of Jesus, or to give people words of encouragement. He is leading people to put their trust in Jesus for themselves, as Son of Man, Christ, Son of God, the Saviour in whom forgiveness is found, the Lord to whom our lives should be given, the

Friend who sticks closer than a brother, and the Leader who takes us out with Him in service to men.

To lead men to Jesus Christ is the supreme aim of our mission. Nothing in the world matters more than that people should know Him for themselves. For this is eternal life: to know the only true God, and Jesus Christ whom He has sent (John 17:3).

(j) He gave them something to do

Jesus did not leave people in the air when they had reached the point of believing in Him.

We have already seen Him telling the paralytic to stand up, take his bed, and go home (Matthew 9:6). He tells the lame man at the Pool of Bethesda to do the same (John 5:8). The lepers whom Jesus healed were told to go and show themselves to the priests, who had the authority to pronounce them clean (Mark 1:44; Luke 17:14).

Although Jesus often told those whom He had healed not to make it known, He did not always do so, and He told the wild man from among the tombs, the Gadarene demoniac, as He is usually called, to go home to his own people and tell them what the Lord in His mercy had done for him (Mark 5:19f.). This man had wanted to follow Jesus into the boat, and the Lord may have felt he must give this man something to do. We can imagine what a long time it would have been since this man had been able to do anything constructive for anyone. Now that he was a new man, there was something he could do: go home and tell.

All these things that we have mentioned were things Jesus gave people to do through which they could bear witness to what He had done for them. There is a danger in inviting people to believe in Christ and leaving it there. Real faith always leads to action, and it is good to suggest to those whom we have been able to lead to faith in Christ quite definite ways in which they can bear witness to this new faith.

Bearing witness to a new-found faith does not necessarily mean preaching to the first members of our family or friends whom we may meet. Parents, in particular, generally dislike intensely being preached at by their children, and some evangelists have created difficult situations by suggesting to young people who have committed themselves to Christ that the first thing they should do is to tell their parents. There are other ways in which the change can be seen.

I remember hearing one man, who is now a Methodist minister, giving his testimony as a candidate for the ministry. After describing his conversion, he went on to say, 'My parents knew that I had been converted, as I began helping with the washing up and brought the coal in.' Jesus had given him something to do to express his new faith.

Quite apart from the instances we have given from the Gospels of something Jesus gave those whom He had recently helped to do, there were many other occasions when he set people to work for Him. Jesus was not the kind of leader who keeps everything in his own hands. He knew that service is a means of grace and He planned ways in which others could help Him. We can imagine the sense of privilege that came to the disciples when He asked them to have a boat ready for him in case the great crowds crushed Him (Mark 3:9), to row

Him across the sea (Mark 4:35f.), to fetch the young donkey on which He was to ride into Jerusalem (Mark 11:1-7), and to prepare the room in which they were to eat the Last Supper (Mark 14:12-16).

In the same way Jesus used others, who may or may not have been disciples, to go ahead of Him into a Samaritan village to make arrangements for Him (Luke 9:51-53), and to roll back the stone at the tomb of Lazarus (John 11:38-40).

We have already, under another heading, referred to the value, on occasion, of asking favours of people who feel they are not wanted. The instances we are looking at now are of a rather different kind. These were the healthy and strong, and Jesus put their health and strength to good use that was a help to Him and a blessing to them.

The ability to delegate responsibility is an important quality of leadership. As F. B. Meyer said, 'It is better to put a hundred men to work than to do the work of a hundred men'. There are Christians who can be encouraged to share in the Church's mission whose gifts at present are not being used and are likely to stagnate. There are people on the fringe of the Church's life whose abilities can be mobilized in the service of the community and who may find it easier to come to know Christ as they serve others than they ever would if they continued to live within the circle of their own family and friends.

It can contribute to the mission of Jesus today, if, like Him, we give people something to do.

(k) He went to His Father for His message and power
The Gospels record a visit of Jesus to His home town

early in His ministry (Matthew 13:53-55). As He taught in their synagogue, the people asked in amazement, 'Where does he get this wisdom from, and these miraculous powers? Is he not the carpenter's son?'

The Fourth Gospel records a similar question asked by the Jews when Jesus had been teaching in the temple (John 7:14-18). 'How is it,' they said, 'that this untrained man has such learning?' Jesus replied, 'The teaching that I give is not my own; it is the teaching of him who sent me. Whoever has the will to do the will of God shall know whether my teaching comes from him or is merely my own.'

Similar statements are made elsewhere in the Fourth Gospel. Jesus said, 'I do not speak on my own authority, but the Father who sent me has himself commanded me what to say and how to speak. I know that his commands are eternal life. What the Father has said to me, therefore—that is what I speak' (John 12:49f.). And again, 'I am not myself the source of the words I speak to you: it is the Father who dwells in me doing his own work' (John 14:10).

Jesus depended on God the Father not only for the words He spoke but also for the power He displayed. When some suggested that it was through the prince of devils that He was driving the devils out, He said, in the course of His reply, 'If it is by the finger of God that I drive out the devils, then be sure the kingdom of God has already come upon you' (Luke 11:20). In Matthew the words used are: 'If it is by the Spirit of God' (Matthew 12:28).

The power Jesus showed, and His dependence on the Spirit of God, are linked together also in the verses that stand at the beginning of Luke's account of His active ministry: 'Then Jesus, armed with the power of the Spirit, returned to Galilee' (Luke 4:14). Again, we are told of the Galilean ministry, 'The power of God was with him to heal the sick' (Luke 5:17).

So Jesus, who was uniquely the Son of God, depended not upon Himself but upon His Father for the words He spoke and for the power He displayed. It is not likely, then, that we shall ever fulfil our task of mission without the same utter dependence on God.

Going to God for our message does not mean sitting in a chair, making our minds go blank, and waiting to see what ideas come into our heads. To understand what the message is with which we are entrusted we need first to study the terms of the commission Jesus gave to His Church between the resurrection and the ascension, and the Christian preparing to engage in the mission of God should consider carefully the passages in which this commission is set out: Matthew 28:16-20; Luke 24:44-49; John 20:19-23, and Acts 1:4-8.

The things that are mentioned in these passages, the things that the members of early Church certainly understood Jesus to have commissioned them to do, are to preach repentance and forgiveness of sins in the name of Jesus Christ, to make disciples, to baptize, and to teach. They were to do this as His witnesses, beginning where they were, but moving away to the ends of the earth, until disciples had been made from all nations.

There is no single item in this programme that is not questioned by some today. There are those who challenge the need to preach repentance and forgiveness on the grounds that the Church has been too morbidly obsessed by sin and guilt, and 'man come of age' can be expected to take no more of it. Others who would believe that there is a place for preaching forgiveness would root it solely in the love of God to the exclusion of the atonement of Christ. Some, as we have seen, regard the aim of making disciples as undue proselytism. Some question the necessity of baptism. Some argue that the role of the Church is not to teach, not, indeed, to verbalize its message at all, but to lose itself, and to be prepared if need be to die, in the fulfilment of its servant role in the world.

We can be sincerely glad that the Church today is being recalled to its servant role and being reminded of the words of Jesus, 'I am among you as one who serves' (Luke 22:27)—words that every Christian should be able to say as he lives his life in the world. But to limit Christian mission to this is to produce a version of Christianity that is not recognizably the one with which the Bible confronts us, and a majority of Christians would not regard any item in the great commission of Jesus as dispensable. We believe that those who profess to be Christians are still expected to fulfil this commission, and always will be.

If there is any reason to think that the fulfilment of this commission is harder than it has been in the past, this only makes it more necessary than ever to emphasize our dependence upon God for our message. As Jesus declared that His words came from the Father, so the Christian must be certain that what he is offering the world as he engages in mission is not some fashionable dish made of ingredients drawn from contemporary philosophy, psychology, and sociology, with a little

97

Christian sauce poured over it, but is the word of God applicable to every age. Each generation may gain new insights into the relevance of this message in the light of man's new discoveries and changing needs, and God has still new light and truth to break forth from His word, but the Christian is not at liberty to omit the essential ingredients of the Christian faith as presented in the Scriptures. And many who have tried to be faithful to the commission that the New Testament tells us Jesus Christ gave to His Church have proved, in what they have seen of the power of the gospel in men's lives, that its terms are still valid today.

In considering the commission of Jesus to His Church, one question arises over which even evangelical Christians are divided, the question whether healing is a part of our commission. Healing men's bodies was a part of the mission of Jesus, and Pentecostals and others are convinced it should be a part of ours. Many other Christians are equally convinced that the healing ministry of God is normally performed in the modern world by the medical profession, and they point out that it is not mentioned in the passages listed earlier in which is set out the commission as the early Church believed it had received it from the lips of Jesus.

The debate on this theme continues, and there is a growing interest in the subject of spiritual healing, even among those who would not see the matter in the same simple terms in which most Pentecostals would see it. Those who believe that this is still a part of the Christian mission point to evidence of the fact of healing in response to faith. Those who argue on the other side point to the danger of being side-tracked from the main themes of the gospel and to the harm done to those who are not healed and who may be given the impression that it is because of a blameworthy lack of faith. Perhaps the truth will be found to lie in a fresh understanding of prayer, of specialized spiritual gifts, as described in I Corinthians 12, of the relation between the mental, physical, and spiritual aspects of man, and of the activity of God in all human processes. Meanwhile, Christians should be wide open to what the Spirit of God may be trying to teach us with regard to the place of healing in mission.

In what we have said about the commission of Jesus our emphasis has been mainly on our dependence upon God for our message. But, like Jesus, we need to go to the Father also for our power. It is of particular encouragement to us to notice an element in the commission of Jesus that we have not so far referred to: His promise of authority and power.

This note is sounded clearly in three of the New Testament summaries of the commission to the Church. In Matthew 28:18-20 are the words, 'Full authority in heaven and on earth has been committed to me. Go forth therefore... And be assured, I am with you always, to the end of time.' In Luke 24:49, Jesus says, 'I am sending upon you my Father's promised gift; so stay here in this city until you are armed with the power from above'. With these words we should read those of Acts 1:4-8: 'You must wait for the promise made by my Father, about which you have heard me speak ... you will be baptized with the Holy Spirit, and within the next few days... You will receive power when the Holy Spirit comes upon you; and you will bear witness for me in Jerusalem, and all over Judaea and Samaria, and away to the ends of the earth.'

To the proposition that we need to depend on the power of the Holy Spirit to do God's work, almost every Christian would be likely to give verbal assent. In every aspect of mission, however, a feeling of being dependent on God can easily give way to a feeling of being able to manage on our own. Every Christian minister, preacher, evangelist, pastor, teacher, counsellor, visitor, social worker, or missionary, unless he is insufferably conceited, is likely to begin his work well aware of his own limitations. But confidence grows with experience, and God-confidence can be replaced by self-confidence. We have done this work before, and people tell us we have done it well, so we know we can do it again.

Not that we are to fall into the opposite mistake of thinking that there is any virtue in feeling inadequate. Christian humility does not, as some people seem to imagine, consist in a conviction that we shall never be any good at anything. Such a conviction does not imply humility so much as lack of faith.

If, as we do God's work, we grow into the right kind of self-confidence, we are much more likely to be effective in the work of mission. The right kind of self-confidence is the kind Paul showed as he wrote, 'I have strength for anything through him who gives me power' (Philippians 4:13), or 'I can do all things in him who strengthens me' (R.S.V.).

To understand more fully what it means to go to God for our message and power we need to ask what it meant for Jesus.

First, it did not mean a lazy lack of preparation for

His work. The ministry of Jesus was prepared for in the hidden years of young manhood before His baptism. It was prepared for also in forty days of wrestling with the implications of His mission during the temptations in the wilderness. And although, not surprisingly, we do not find recorded in the Gospels any account of His preparation for what He was going to say to the crowds, His teaching does not, except where He is giving a quick answer to a question, give the impression of off-the-cuff comment. The parables show every evidence of having been carefully thought out. The way in which almost all His recorded sayings are clothed in similes or metaphors, or in some striking and even startling form, suggests that not only the thoughts being expressed but the way in which they were to be expressed had been turned over in the mind of Jesus before He spoke.

The words of reassurance that Jesus spoke in Matthew 10:19f., 'Do not worry about what you are to say; when the time comes, the words you need will be given you; for it is not you who will be speaking: it will be the Spirit of your Father speaking in you', were said in a context of coming persecution. They are preceded by the words 'When you are arrested', and we may be sure they were never intended, as a few have thought, to justify lack of preparation on the part of the Christian preacher. To share in God's communication to men is a privilege and responsibility so great that it deserves the best that careful preparation can give.

Second, going to God for His message and for His power meant for Jesus setting aside time for quiet communion with His Father. We do not, of course, know anything directly of the content of His thought and prayer during times such as those mentioned in Luke 4:42, 5:16, and 6:12, though sometimes it is possible to infer from the context what particular issue He may have wanted to think and pray through at times like those. We must not imply that they were times primarily of what we would call 'sermon preparation', but what we can say is that an element in the background of Jesus' dependence on God for His message and power was the communion He enjoyed in these hours when He withdrew from men. And if He needed such times, we are not likely to need them less. For the Christian engaged in mission there is no substitute for a quiet time with God.

What Christian spirituality should mean today is much under discussion among Christian thinkers. We may have been over-legalistic in the past and have gone beyond what can be shown from Scripture as to the time the Christian should spend in prayer and the best time of day to meet with God. There are no rigid rules for this, and we have not always remembered that Jesus told men not to be like the heathen who imagine that the more they say the more likely they are to be heard (Matthew 6:7).

There is certainly room for a fresh look at what spirituality should be expected to mean for the Christian. But as we take that fresh look we need to remember that our inborn laziness is likely to snatch at any excuse for reducing what is expected of us, and that the devaluation of prayer is an almost inevitable accompaniment to the process of secularization that is going on at an accelerating pace, and may be one of its most unwelcome features.

Without prayer there is a vacuum in man, and the exploration of Eastern techniques of meditation by a small but growing number is a sign that the vacuum is there. From techniques of meditation the Christian may have something to learn, but for him a possibility far more helpful than mere meditation is open: the possibility of being in daily touch with the Living God. And if he is to share in the mission of Jesus in any form or at any level he needs to go to God for his message and power, and the best way to do this is by setting aside times for communion with Him.

For many Christians it is indeed the demands of mission, understood in the wider sense in which we have defined it, that keep them alert to the fact that they are 'standing in the need of prayer'. Asking people to read their Bibles and say their prayers leaves many cold. But if we ask them to do some work for God their sense of inadequacy will often drive them to prayer. In order to give out, whether it is in evangelism or demanding service, they may see at last their need to take in.

This is the pattern of healthy Christian life: taking in and giving out. If we give out without taking in, we are drained dry. If we take in without giving out, we soon reach saturation point. Jesus was giving out daily, and daily He needed to take in. And if the ordinary Christian is fulfilling his role in the world as an ambassador of Christ, he, too, is giving out daily, and daily he needs to take in.

There is one final thing that we must add about the way Jesus went to God for His message and His power. We have written a good deal about the special times of communion Jesus enjoyed with His Father. But this is not the whole story. 'I am in the Father and the Father in me,' He is reported as saying to His disciples (John 14:11). He went to God for His message and power not only in set times of prayer but in a moment-by-moment walk with God. Not only at the crisis-points of His life but at any time of the night or day the lines were clear for Him.

That God is always on the line for us also is axiomatic for the Christian, but we do not always practise the presence of God that is ours to enjoy. Soon after the words we quoted from John 14, Jesus said something that drew the disciples right into this unbroken communion with His Father about which He had spoken. Not only did He say, 'I am in the Father and the Father in me', but also, 'I am in my Father, and you in me and I in you' (John 14:20). Their task was to bear fruit, and this they could do if they dwelt in Him, as He in them (John 15:4).

Here is the statement that makes all the challenging demands of mission possible to us, for we, too, can go to God for our message and our power. The Holy Spirit is ours also. The parson in his pulpit, the missionary nurse in her hospital, the layman on the factory floor, the national Christian serving his community in one of the developing countries, the pensioner talking to her neighbour over the garden fence, the newly-committed teenager fumbling his way into witness at school, the lonely Christian in an unbelieving home, all of them can know that this is true for them.

'I can do all things in him who strengthens me.'

Index of Scripture References